THE ART OF CORPORATE WARFARE

How to Change Your Approach and Kick Ass Every Day

Tal Newhart

Copyright 2015 Tal Newhart
All rights reserved. No part of this book may be reproduced in any format, print or electronic, without permission in writing from the copyright holder.

www.linkedin.com/in/talnewhart

ISBN: 1519439075
ISBN 13: 9781519439079

DEDICATION

This book is dedicated to my clients and readers who, over the course of many years, have encouraged me to assemble my most popular and useful postings into something that can be used as a manual for beating up their competition. Thanks for the push. Now, go kick some ass...everyday!

CONTENTS

Dedication		iii
Introduction		ix
A Note about Corpcraft		xvii
Chapter 1	The "Plan with Branches"	1
Chapter 2	Mistakes—And What Great Leaders Do About Them	6
Chapter 3	Avoiding Defeat Caused by Victory	9
Chapter 4	Six Traits of a Good Manager	12
Chapter 5	Winning or Losing with Near Certainty	16
Chapter 6	Concentration of Force	19
Chapter 7	The Risk of "Normal Innovation"	22
Chapter 8	About Generals and CEOs	29
Chapter 9	Controlling Napoleon	31
Chapter 10	Avoiding Your Own Charge of the Light Brigade	33

Chapter 11	Lucius Quinctius Cincinnatus: The Perfect Leader?	42
Chapter 12	A CEO Talks about the Importance of Grokking	46
Chapter 13	A Reader's Strategy—Act Like a Snake	49
Chapter 14	Getting Ahead Through Fakery	51
Chapter 15	How to Avoid Your Own Waterloo	54
Chapter 16	What We Seem to be Forgetting & Why We're in Trouble	62
Chapter 17	The Key Trait of a True Corporate Warrior	66
Chapter 18	"The Feint": Genghis Khan and Henry Kravis—Different Time, Same Tactic	77
Chapter 19	How a Famous CEO Stays so Calm	80
Chapter 20	Preventing Systemic Failure (Things to Look Out For)	87
Chapter 21	Upturning, in a Downturn	91
Chapter 22	Pressuring Generals (CEOs) to disclose their plans. Wrong!	95
Chapter 23	Bill Swanson's "25 Unwritten Rules of Management"	98
Chapter 24	Normal vs. Extraordinary Performance (vs. Vanity)	103
Chapter 25	Holiday Comments about Corporate Responsibility	105
Chapter 26	"Capitalist Gone Wild!!"	110
Chapter 27	A Useful Business Weapon Called FUD	114

Chapter 28	FUD Update	119
Chapter 29	More lessons from the Corporate Battlefield with Client X	125
Chapter 30	Some Basic Rules of Corporate Warfare	133
Chapter 31	How a Fortune 500 CEO Helps Change Happen in 7 Steps	137

Addendum: Some Interesting and Useful Interviews	143
The Ethical Hacker Interview	145
What You Should be Doing Minute to Minute	155
What's Your Stirrup?	158
Advice from a Mysterious Russian	162
Ensuring Corporate Victory by Using OODA Loops	169
About Tal Newhart & The Art of Corporate Warfare	173

INTRODUCTION

"All wars are won, or lost, before they are fought."

–Sun Tzu

And that, folks, is what this manual is all about: A toolkit for winning marketplace battles.

Sun Tzu, arguably one of the greatest generals in history, said a great general (e.g. a great CEO which is largely the same thing) puts his army (employees) beyond the possibility of defeat.

I have spent many years in the high-end human capital and project management business. As a student of military history I realized early on in my entrepreneurial and recruiting careers that the best senior level executives think a lot like history's great generals

(Scipio Africanus, Sun Tzu, Genghis Khan, Napoleon, Alexander the Great, the war strategist Carl von Clausewitz, etc. The list is long.). I also realized that classic basic battle tactics and techniques were easily adapted to the modern business landscape. And, furthermore, that the tactics could be frighteningly effective at marginalizing or even neutralizing a more powerful, better funded, competitor (watching military veterans do this can be a thing of beauty). I discovered if you have a practical knowledge of battle tactics, and your competition doesn't, you have an asymmetry of power with you holding the bigger axe. You just have to decide if you want to swing it since sometimes it's enough to simply be seen holding the thing. And, of course, it might be the real thing, or it might look like the real thing, but actually be made out of paper mâché—that'll be your secret. The point is if they think it's real, well, you are controlling their perceived reality and that's great. That's The Art of Corporate Warfare. Fun, isn't it?

The fact is what most superior chief-level managers understand, on some level, is that corporate competition is a form of warfare. Civilized, hopefully, but warfare nonetheless, like it or not. An experienced entrepreneur or business leader understands this because most have seen the wake of corporate battles lost. They have seen, not just the nasty wreckage losing creates for them personally, but also the devastation business reversals can cause to a company's workers and their families (functionally the workers are the CEO's army) and ultimately the equity holders (the equity holders are the CEO/general's civilian population). This is an important reason why a great general or CEO wants to win. It's too expensive to lose.

One of the interesting things that happened when my Art of Corporate Warfare newsletter became popular, not long after 9/11, was a certain fraction of readers pushed back very hard on the whole idea that business and war were basically the same thing and only the stakes are different. You could describe some of the reactions as moral outrage that I would dare to compare a "real war" with something that happens in the perceived antiseptic environment of corporate competition. This attitude never worked for me since I routinely saw families economically shattered because the breadwinner's employer got bested in the marketplace. You witness that emotional devastation as much as I did and winning takes on a whole new meaning with niceties kicked to the nearest grubby curb. Then there's the self-doubt that can't help but creep into an entrepreneur, the big bore engines of any growing economy, when they fail.

When I reached out to a sample of the disapproving group I found that very few were blood war vets who understand emotional strain and loss on a level few non-vets can even begin to understand. No, the naysayers were mostly readers simply moribund in their jobs. They were corpses with a pulse. They were stuck and, if they didn't change the way they thought, would always be stuck. From their myopic, slacker perspective they were the worn gears of some uncaring machine that continued to slowly crank away, grinding down the souls of its weakest human parts, including themselves.

That's a grim perspective but, let's face it, big machines need parts to function and generate value. If you are one of these parts, clearly valuable because you are being paid, embrace it if you can't change it. You may be fungible (which ultimately everyone is) but that doesn't mean the company doesn't need you. Don't just simply bitch about it. It's simple, really: fix it or shut up and if the only way you can shut up is to leave then, well, see ya!

The group of people content to just bitch or suffer in silence and wallow in self- pity are seriously not-my-audience, LOL.

These people are not "corporate warriors". If the wallowers have no real interest in making some change to increase shareholder equity, even if it's just by a little, then I have no interest in helping them. Period. My newsletter was always like leading a horse to water. Most of the readers drank well, sometimes insatiably, (especially the thankful entrepreneurs who often compared the newsletter to taking a machinegun to a knife fight). But if the horse had no interest in the water then fine. I figured that's what buzzards were for.

CEOs, senior managers and people doing start-ups, however, typically embrace the whole Corpwar ethos.

The Art of Corporate Warfare

They get it. They don't expect anything to be easy. The good ones know battle, in any form, is not for the squeamish. They know battles happen, you just have to be better than the other guy because you need to win.

It is essential to understand that traditional war and fierce business competition are largely the same thing. Generally speaking, somebody has something you want and they don't want to give it to you at a "price" you are willing to pay. So, if you really want it, you have to take it. This is speaking symbolically but hopefully you get the point. And, if you engage to take it, you have to win because losing sucks for all kinds of reasons, including the simple fact losing is expensive in so many ways. So battle, whether it's a blood war in Afghanistan, or a battle for shampoo market share, is about the same thing. It's about WINNING. Winning in the least amount of time, at the lowest possible cost, and for the greatest reward possible. Pretty simple. It's what you get a paycheck to do. You don't get paid to lose. You get paid to win.

If you get that, if you really understand it, and embrace it, then you are already on the path to being a true corporate warrior who, by definition, "does what it takes" to add value to the enterprise employing them. That's why people like me look so hard for people like them. Corporate warriors, at any place on the org chart, are the tornadic winds that drive relevant improvement in their part of the organization. In the case of the CEO or entrepreneur, it's the whole organization.

Look back at history's great battles through an open mental lens and you will see there is a lot to learn about ridding yourself of a competitor. It's basic. You want them gone. They don't want to go. Or they want you gone. But you don't want to go. Pretty basic. Ask any soldier.

Welcome to war. If the analogy doesn't work for you then you're at the wrong party. Go get another book. One of those touchy feely "simple" ways-to-get-ahead books at the airport bookshop. Enjoy yourself and good luck with that bright red bulls-eye on your back.

But if you are willing to do what it takes to win then this book provides some very useful tools. Not all by any stretch, but some very important ones you're unlikely to find collected elsewhere. These tools range from techniques based on historical battles (e.g. Waterloo, The Charge of the Light Brigade, Khan's tactics, etc.) to personal techniques and philosophies passed along to me by clients, candidates and friends over the years. A lot of what I learned is in this collection. Some of it is tough. So what.

Ultimately what it all gets down to is creating sustainable increases in the value of the business and, that done, maybe even help improve society and the environment. That's what a corporate warrior does. And this book will help you do this if you keep some of the lessons front of mind, like asking yourself a few times a day "What is the most important thing I can be doing

RIGHT NOW to improve our business?" Or, "How can I control the movements of my competition by adjusting their perception of my condition or intentions?" Or, simply, "What would Alexander the Great do?" (Answer: He would think outside the box and there's a useful example in this collection.)

And throughout, try and have fun. You can't tell kids this, but more seasoned readers will understand: "Life is short." So have fun. Mess with the head of your counterpart. Fiddle with them. Stick your foot out and watch them trip over it. That's cool. Enjoy it because if they could do the same thing to you they would, but you thought of it first. So you get to do the laughing. If that sounds too harsh, well, you know the drill: Get another book.

Think about it…
 Now, go beat up your competition. Go win.

Tal Newhart
TalNewhart.com
Chicago

A required note on the contents
Many of the conversations, interviews and shared experiences detailed in this collection were originally published under strict

terms of confidentiality in perpetuity. Some of the clearances took over a year to obtain with clients, et al. who were given the provisional right to reasonably redact and/or change the content in order to gain their comfort and permission. In certain cases the changes were significant enough for me to decline to publish the final version. Those were tossed…thanks for the memories. What remains in the collection is pretty much what was said, largely verbatim off recordings, or from in situ notes detailing what was actually said and done at the time. Even the aggressive stuff.

A NOTE ABOUT CORPCRAFT

"Corpcraft" is a term I came up with early on in my career as a recruiter and entrepreneur. It is a sort of shorthand I used with my team and it naturally, over the years, found its way into occasional use in The Art of Corporate Warfare newsletter.

Used correctly the term is efficient and telling. When an executive displays good corpcraft they are making a wide variety of decisions that result in a sustainable increase in equity holder value. In my perspective that's what it all comes down to. Enhancing social and environmental conditions are important as well, but most equity holders view those as somewhat secondary to more easily quantifiable self-interest.

When we do executive searches, along with good "fit" into the new organization, truly proven corpcraft is a large part of what we are looking for in candidates. When we are looking for acquisition targets for clients, the presence of good corpcraft is, likewise, a vital variable. In both cases the entities of interest consistently make "good" decisions, often leveraging less obvious techniques and philosophies, and are always focused on moving the enterprise ahead in a sustainable manner.

Corpcraft, at its poorest, is reflected in equity holder disasters like those of Enron, WorldCom, etc. and are typically brought on by people and/or boards that have a fatally impaired sense of the future. An important aspect of individuals and companies with poor corpcraft is that they are generally fairly easy targets for mitigation or elimination because they help bring it on themselves. An individual or organization lacking corpcraft is like a deer in the headlights of someone that has it. Also, I've frequently observed over the years that those that possess good corpcraft find identifying where it's lacking to often be a humorously trivial matter.

Think about it…

CHAPTER 1

THE "PLAN WITH BRANCHES"

Originally Published
September 2010

(From the competitive playbooks of Genghis Khan and Napoleon)

"The nature of strategy consists of always having, even with a weaker army (company), more forces at the point of attack than the enemy."

-Napoleon Bonaparte

I had an interesting conversation last week with a European CEO of a mid-cap manufacturing company.

He had been mentioned in the Wall Street Journal wherein he described a convoluted recovery scheme that the editorial tone suggested was both brash and nouveau. But I thought I recognized it for what it was: brilliant and quite old. Since he reads this column I called and asked him if my hunch was right and he laughed and reported that, indeed, it was. What follows is the military history. It's not hard to see the application to modern business as a way to provoke your competition into making foolish, exploitable moves. It's all about control.

The tactic's first recorded use was by Genghis Khan and his Mongol general Subedei Bahadur in 1241. Like Genghis Kahn, Subedei was a brilliant and innovative strategist. He sent four distinct troop columns into Europe. One headed directly for Poland and Germany which attracted all the European military forces in that direction. This is exactly what Subedei wanted. The other three columns entered Hungary in an indistinct fashion attacking various targets all while focusing on keeping the Austrian forces from combining with the Hungarian. That was the actual agenda—keep the enemy forces apart. When the time was right the three Mongol columns then magically combined into one large force and shattered the unsupported Hungarian forces.

It was brilliant back then. And remains so. The key in all competition (war, business, etc.) is to avoid, or mitigate, your competition's strengths and exploit their weaknesses.* The Mongol Subedei could quickly combine forces to focus on exploitable weakness in a way a large, unwieldy force couldn't. War is largely about real estate so this is a great advantage. By having multiple forces the Mongol could control the movements of his enemy by forcing them to spread out to defend multiple targets. This numerically weakened the individual targets' defenses making it easier (read: less costly) to attack them. Prevent your numerically superior competition from concentrating its forces against you. Then divide and conquer them. I covered this in the piece about Southwest Airlines elsewhere in this collection.

If you are skillful enough you can force your opponent to protect itself so thinly that they abandon their position in order to survive elsewhere. This is war in the best Sun Tzu tradition of winning with little or no fighting. This tactic could, for example, lead to a favorable corporate merger when previously none was possible.

Napoleon advanced the tactic using what has been called the "weighted net." Napoleon would send out numerous columns where, like a waving net, they would focus on various threats and speedily envelope the useful or dangerous ones. Then move on. This confused his enemies who would try to coalesce for an offensive attack on something that looked weak, but would suddenly find Napoleon's forces massing more efficiently elsewhere, and then attacking with superior strength, before the enemy could effectively combine. In effect

Napoleon would direct his forces to act like an octopus with waving arms. When one arm sensed something of value the other arms would suddenly be brought into play to deal with the opportunity. When finished they would separate to look for new opportunities. Elegant, effective stuff.

So, what's the point? The point is that even a large, well-financed competitor can't optimally protect all of its markets, all of the time. By dividing your forces you can confuse your target and cause them to think your approach is coming from a different direction with a different intent, hiding your actual objective. Done correctly this can cause your (hopefully) unenlightened competition to expend resources to protect the incorrect target (think product or service), weakening support for your actual objective. This opens the door for you. Never forget that frontal attacks against hardened targets are seldom successful and always expensive.

Think about it...

Notes: This is a variation of the feint, which is discussed elsewhere. It's another method of controlling your enemy/competition through an elaborate form of deception. Never forget that, used intelligently, deception makes war (competition) less costly and reduces risk. All the Great generals have known this.

The phrase "plan with branches" was coined in the late eighteenth century by French strategist Pierre de Bourcet.

---

*This is why you have to spend part of every day asking yourself, "Has our competition's strengths changed and are there any new weaknesses we can now exploit?" Your stakeholders EXPECT you to think this way. You're paid to do it.

CHAPTER 2

MISTAKES—AND WHAT GREAT LEADERS DO ABOUT THEM

Originally Published
March 2008

> *"If everyone is thinking alike,
> somebody isn't thinking."*
>
> *-General George Patton, Jr.*

Genghis Kahn was always trying new ways to capture new ground. This is one reason he created an empire on a scale never seen before, or since. He would try something new and unexpected, and this would throw off his enemy. After all, it was new!

But, like any manager that is pushing the envelope, he knew there would be some failures. He would make mistakes. The key was that he encouraged discourse about them. He was not so wrapped up in his own superiority that he wouldn't listen. Like any great general, or CEO, Khan actively removed impediments to the truth reaching him. Great leaders know they don't know it all. Their greatness comes, in part, from creating open, sharing environments. They know it takes more than best practices—everybody wants to talk about those. A true leader ensures he knows about the organization's "worst practices" as well. Why? Because they know if you can't see it…you can't fix it.

So you have to ask yourself: "If I am aware of a mistake, what do I do? If one of my team makes a mistake what will they expect my reaction will be when I find out? And, typically, how do I find out?" Genghis Khan and his chief orloks, Subedei and Jebe (an orlok was a marshal) would sit around the smoky yurt (not much wood on the steppes so they burned dung) and talk about what tactics worked that day and what didn't (although appearing chaotic, Mongol tactics were precisely engineered in advance). Occasional failure was an accepted cost of moving forward. Not admitting that a mistake had occurred meant someone in the vast organization might make the mistake again and they knew that was counterproductive; an unnecessary expense.

So admitting to a mistake was the important, group oriented thing to do. Mistakes are always costly in some way—but you get a rebate by learning from them. And sometimes a big bonus...

One advantage of scrutinizing seemingly minor mistakes is because they can be precursors to disasters. Big organizational disasters, and Khan had only a few, almost always have weak inflection points somewhere in the event stream leading to the catastrophe. It doesn't take much to imagine Khan and his orloks sitting around studying each mistake so it didn't lead to a bigger one, which would in turn cause another, etc. Soon you have Enron or New Coke or Bear Stearns when somebody could easily have broken the chain. Corporate warriors never forget, big, sprawling mistakes don't just happen. They *evolve*.

You can't have your people hiding problems. You need to ask yourself: Do people around you in your organization hide the bad news from you? If so, why? What are they afraid of? Is it you personally, or the corporate culture? If either, you have repairs to make.

Finally, Khan knew that, as the leader (and this applies to any manager), it was imperative that he admit when he possibly made a mistake. If he didn't, who would? Khan knew a fish smells from the head first.

Think about it...

CHAPTER 3

AVOIDING DEFEAT CAUSED BY VICTORY

Originally Published
April 2007

It's been said that one of the greatest causes of defeat on the battlefield, or in business, is simply victory. We often see this in sports teams, too. The team gets thoroughly psyched up to trounce a tougher opponent, succeeds brilliantly, and then promptly gets beaten by a lesser adversary. Good managers, like good coaches and generals, know about this and plan for it. With each victory they don't relax, but take it up a notch. It's as important as continuous improvement, but not as fluid. The philosophical cartography of an aggressive, equity holder-centric team, needs both.

Sun Tzu, clearly one of the greatest "team" leaders (military, sports or business is beside the point) in history, made a point of always exploiting his own victories. He did this because he considered not doing so was to have wasted the consumed resources. It's useful to remember that any honest general (from Sun Tzu to the present) knows that no war is best. Unfortunately that's not always practical and occasionally you have to engage in military or commercial carnage. Because wars are expensive, in so many ways, the key is to keep the conflict short. Short wars are better than long ones. Always. And don't fight if you know you can't win. That's just stupid. Ask Donald Trump.

One of Sun Tzu's key shortening strategies was to consolidate his gains, or, to put it another way, constantly build on his successes. Big ones. Little ones. All of them. After all, you are motivated to achieve a success for a reason that materially improves you, otherwise why do it (ego is not a good reason)? You exit the success with the value to the stakeholders somehow improved, which is the object of the exercise.

So, it's always about taking your achieved victory and using it to methodically bump up your baseline. Always asking yourself, "Ok, we're a bit better now. How can we exploit our new state and move up to the next level?" Just keep hammering away. Make it a habit; part of your natural thought process. A subtle breeze in a sand desert will eventually wear away a solid building.

This relentless incremental movement forward has some interesting side benefits as well. Like Sun Tzu,

Russian military strategist Carl von Clausewitz emphasized the importance of unambiguously demonstrating your resolve for victory. The constant leveraging of your own victory, for more victory, is a vivid psychological signal to your competition. It says, "Sure, you can try, but it's going to be costly so you had better be very sure."

So winning can't be an isolated incident. You have to sustain it by expanding upon it each and every time it happens. The corporate world is full of individuals and companies that arced victoriously through the commercial sky only to quickly fade away because they forgot to keep building on their success, forgot to always be planning and moving ahead.

The stark reality is, transient victory aside, the moment you stop getting stronger, you start getting weaker. And getting weaker is the beginning of dying. And then you're dead.

And you'll deserve it because you didn't see the hungry eyes in the trees, waiting.

Think about it…

CHAPTER 4

SIX TRAITS OF A GOOD MANAGER

From a Podcast
Super Bowl Sunday, 2006

I came down to Cuernavaca, Mexico to interview a candidate for a one-year operations assignment seated in Europe. In the course of the interview I asked the candidate what he felt the components of a good leader are (this was one of the questions the CEO wanted us to ask in addition to our usual Q deck), basically, the candidate's take on the traits of good leadership. The question was asked within the context of what he would be tasked to do if he was hired, and that was to open up a new supply chain in Europe. He broke it down to the six traits he typically looks for when hiring people that report to him. He clarified that these traits focus "inwardly on the management team" rather than outward into the realm of client advocacy which he felt equally as strongly about.

As you review the list you can see Carlos' overarching theme is to make sure everyone in the organization understands they must strive to somehow add more value to the organization and its customers, thus increasing the company's value in both financial and social terms. He constantly challenged his employees to ask themselves "How can I add more value?" and to ask themselves that question at least once every day.

The Traits & Related Behaviors

1. **Being able to make a decision.** Good managers are like good generals—they can make decisions. Sometimes the suggestions come from team members and smart internal advisors, but often the decisions come from that mysterious place inside true leaders. Good managers slice through all the minutia and make a decision. Nothing happens without a decision. Even doing nothing is a decision. Carlos said the problem with the latter is that doing nothing is often so comfortable. But if you're doing nothing, you're probably standing still and that's when your competition will run you over. Also, accept responsibility for

your decisions whether or not they turn out to be right or wrong. Learn from your mistakes.
2. **Be a good role model.** Never forget, in one respect business organizations are no different from fish: they both start to smell bad from the head down. Be consistent to the company's philosophy. Talk is cheap, actions count. As the leader, people will gravitate to, and emulate, your behavior. It always has to point toward creating sustainable increases in equity holder value while hopefully supporting sound social values as well.
3. **Focus.** Good leaders pick out the most important thing and that's what they do. Once that's done, they move on to the next, then the next.
4. **Being there.** Don't just sit behind your desk. Get out there to your employees and customers. Let people know that you know what's going on and that you care. Great managers aren't detached. They get out there and are symbolically on the shop floor.
5. **Give positive feedback to their team members.** Always be net positive. When he had to be critical Carlos would think it out and try to be just as honest in his criticism as he was complimentary. This helped his team members trust what he had to say.
6. **Always move forward.** Always stay dynamic. Stay optimistic and continually make things better.

A complacent manager is doomed. A great enterprise never "arrives" anywhere; it's always in motion. Be like the Eveready bunny—just keep going and going and going. "A good manager will always strive to reach the horizon even though he knows he can never arrive."

Think about it...

CHAPTER 5

WINNING OR LOSING WITH NEAR CERTAINTY

Originally Published
April 2008

> *"Battles are won or lost before they are fought."*
>
> *–Sun Tzu*

Last week I received a phone call from a longtime reader that is out of work and asked me if I knew of anything (we keep both formal and informal lists of readers looking for fellow hard hitters). As a rule I'm sympathetic to involuntary unemployment since I know what it can do to a family. So I listened. A moment later

I connected the name to the news and I tightened up. Although it was announced he had "resigned for personal reasons" everybody knows he was fired because of the poor performance of his company. I asked him what happened. He very articulately explained what I already knew because it had been given a lot of coverage in the financial press. I also looked up the stock price while he was on the phone—it was all right there. He described how every time they (the company) went into a new market they were trounced, or nearly trounced, by the incumbent. "Suddenly they would deploy all these resources we had no clue they had. Nobody knew." Huh? I mean seriously…*what?*

Please. This guy deserved to be fired. If he was a military general in the battlefield, rather than a civilian one hiding away in his corner office, sons and daughters would be gone. A lot of them. I couldn't get off the phone fast enough. A weak whiner. No wonder his company's expensive efforts were so easy to defeat. All that equity holder value wasted. Poof!

Never forget: "Battles are won or lost before they are fought." Although it came from Sun Tzu a very long time ago there is absolutely nothing mysterious and illusive about this. The reader's comment about "Nobody knew" is just plain lame—a genuinely ludicrous excuse for egregiously poor chief-level performance. Everybody in the other companies knew what was available to deploy against a new manufacturer entering their market spaces. The defeated guy on the phone was surprised when he should have been prepared for marketplace battle. His idea of being prepared for the worst, was expecting the best, and that's what he provisioned for. And this happened to his company more than once! He should have been fired 8 years ago. I'm embarrassed the guy is a reader of this newsletter. It makes me feel like I've somehow failed.

Remember, the outcome is always decided before the clash. Business. War. Parenting. It's all the same, folks. Only the stakes are different.

And this works all the way down through your company. Everybody in your company, including those in your department, should think like a good soldier. Always ask yourself what's the worst that can happen within the timeframe relevant to your job scope. The shipping clerk's horizon is different than the CEO's but The Magic Question is the same: "What can go dreadfully wrong and what have I done to prepare myself, and my team, for it?"

That's only one part of earning your paycheck and supporting your equity holders, but it's a vitally important one.

"If you know the enemy and know yourself, you need not fear the result of a hundred battles. If you know yourself but not the enemy, for every victory gained you will also suffer a defeat. If you know neither the enemy nor yourself, you will succumb in every battle."- Sun Tzu

Think about it...

CHAPTER 6

CONCENTRATION OF FORCE

**Originally Published
March 2003**

> *"The law of successful operations is to avoid the enemy's strength and strike at his weakness."*
>
> –Sun Tzu

Concentration of force is one of the great principals of successful battle. Alexander of Macedon (a.k.a. Alexander the Great) and Napoleon both employed it. It's also very effective in business—and can be savagely effective for "the little guy" with limited resources. That

David fella knew just what to do when Goliath came along—aim for the weakness. Herb Kelleher did the same thing with Southwest Airlines.

The key is to look for weakness in your opponent's strengths then engineer a relative superiority (e.g. like Keller did). You then apply the strength against your competitor's weakness (making sure it's a TRUE weakness, and not just clever bait—ouch!). Napoleon was brilliant in his ability to actually create the weakness in the enemy's line using skillful maneuvering, and not necessarily superior firepower (e.g. using cleverness instead of committing capital). Then he would drive through. It was first employed by Alexander the Great 2,000 years before who used it to repeatedly defeat the decidedly less clever Persian leader Darius.

We used this around here, of course. When we started out again after selling JobPlex.com we were just another small recruiting service. But we studied, then specialized in "high-speed/high-impact search" (e.g. clients could come to us to quickly marginalize their competition by having us use our competitor intelligence skills to first identify, and then dutifully extract, valuable talent from a worrisome competitor). This focus, this concentration of energy, gave us a tremendous advantage over our entrenched, slow-moving competition. As the market caught up, we then moved onto more interesting specialties and services.

By thinking like this, smart small-guys like Southwest Airlines and many others have been happily poking javelins at the rear end of big guys for thousands of years.

You can too. Ask yourself, what are my competitor's true weaknesses and does it make solid sense to attack there? The notion of 'true weakness' needs to be emphasized since really tough, knowledgeable competitors will create lures and wait for you to fall for them. Don't do that unless it's part of a broader, carefully engineered strategy.

And if you think it's beginning to feel a bit like a game of chess, then you're getting it.

Think about it…

CHAPTER 7

THE RISK OF "NORMAL INNOVATION"

Originally Published
November 2011

And what to do about it

The Gordian Knot, presented to Alexander the Great in 333 B.C., has become symbolic of an unsolvable puzzle. History suggests it may have been an actual knot, impossible to untie. In fact it wasn't until recently when Polish physicist Piotr Pieranski wrote a knot program* called SOTOS that the knot was finally undone. It turned out not to be a knot at all (note: when Alexander was presented with the challenge no rope ends were visible) but rather a loop of rope (2 ends spliced together) that was probably wetted, somehow entangled, and then shrunk in the sun. With insufficient looseness it would have been impossible to unravel the rope.

However, Alexander the Great was innovative and had an interesting solution to "luein" (loosen/solve) the knot. After all, Zeus had said anybody that could undo the knot would rule all of Asia. Thusly motivated Alexander stared at the twisted mass for a while, then abruptly took out his sword and sliced the knot in half. Nobody had thought of that solution before. But that was ok. After all, the challenge was to "part the knot". The how was left to the attempter. It wasn't how he played the game—it was whether he won or lost.

Result: Problem solved by looking at it differently than others. And, of course, Alexander went on to rule Asia.

Alexander knew how to innovate.

Alexander the Great was known as a great innovator in matters of war and competition. Napoleon was using Alexander's techniques a thousand years later and they still worked (well, except that last time…).

Alexander looked for different ways to do things. For example, Alexander was the first to use the "strike at the weak spot" strategy. It seems simple and obvious now but in 334 B.C. it had never been formalized and he used it to shatter more powerful, better equipped armies. Never satisfied, he then refined it by cleverly creating a weak spot in the enemy line, then attacking there.

How? Simple if you look beyond the obvious. Alexander knew the enemy (his competition) was always watching him. He realized he could cause the enemy to physically move around by rearranging his own men. Using this, Alexander would, by moving his men, carefully have the enemy arrange itself in a manner that would ensure its own defeat. This led to less costly victories for Alexander and in war cheaper, with good results, is always better. This is why smart generals/CEOs/managers are always asking themselves, "How can I control my competition?" This makes competition cheaper and thus better for our equity holders. It's fun too.

However, in the example, you need to look carefully at what Alexander did in the battlefield. It has two parts. One was the pure innovation (strike at the weak spot), the second was a refinement (create the weak spot in the first place)—the second was a sustaining move on the previous innovation. Don't confuse them.

One of the definitions of a well-managed company is one that carefully listens to its customers and provides what they want. Super performing companies do this better than their competition via a sort of hyper-alignment with their clients.

But this extreme client centricity relative to innovation does carry a risk. You are thinking inside the box (e.g. the client's). And if you are doing a good job you are probably receiving rewards and that feels good in all sorts of ways. But you probably aren't truly innovating. You must objectively examine your actions and see if you are really just sustaining, in some fashion, an existing product or service (even if it's "new"). There's a difference and the difference can doom even a great company.

How? Even if you are performing greatly you have to ask yourself what you will do if somebody comes along with a client usable solution that is so different that you never even thought of it. Your client never thought of it either. In fact, maybe nobody but the goofy guy in the fabled garage, or some small market "skunk works", ever thought of it. But it works better than your solution. And your clients gravitate to that new solution because that's what their equity holders expect them to do—wouldn't you? (Have you ever noticed how often small cap skunk works often smell like money? It's an invigorating odor, even if it can occasionally smell like people have forgotten how to bathe...).

What makes this especially grim is, on the surface, you're being penalized for being a "good", well-managed company. You listened and were guided by your clients. Maybe you even took a bit of a chance and got out in front of them—helped them see a marginally better way. Even improved them. Companies win awards for doing that.

However, in many cases what we're doing with that innovation, without knowing it, is simply treading water. Looking at the knot the same old way. In fact some of your well-intentioned, engineering driven, innovation may simply be "over-satisfying" the client's need and that's not helpful to your equity holders. In fact it can be damaging because you are diverging from what your client actually needs and wants to pay for. Less can be more. Eventually customers learn this.

The point is although you are admirably aligned with your clients you are still at risk because your client will switch away from you if a better way comes along. They have to.

Find your industry's Gordian Knot. Then untie it.
The challenge is to also venture outside the often small and constricting, client-driven, innovation box. Really do it. A lot of us think we do it, but we don't. Not really. Why? Frankly, it's a strange place for a traditionally well-run company. Too many unknowns. Somebody will ask you, "But what's the ROI going to be?" Huh? You can't analyze what doesn't exist. True innovation, the real fresh stuff that flips your industry on its ear, is a financial analysis black hole. I know many CFOs and they have it tough enough already. Black holes? "No thanks."

But you have to do it. Some call it "disruptive technology." That's a bit pop for my tastes but the idea is there. And I agree with it. It is, after all, the polar of merely sustaining and that's risky. It speaks to the notion that you can't get stuck—sometimes you have to just throw away what you call normal.

Whatever you label it, figure out how you are going to pay for it and who is going to do it. Then give them some space and stand back. If it were me I'd tell them to come up with the industry's Gordian Knot and when they came up with it I'd tell them, "Great, now go figure out how to untie it. Or find the guy or gal in the garage that may already know. Take a checkbook. Get going!"

Is the approach too weird? Too expensive? Then create an internal mechanism (preferably an accountable person or small group—and yes, it may be a peculiar job description) whose job it is to know about anything (ANYTHING!) that can cause your customers to do things differently. Why? Because if they start doing things differently they may not do them with you. And this has killed off many a "great" company.

I once had a plaque made for my office wall. It said: "A company exists to create customers." As I'm older now I think I should add: "and keep them for a long, long time." Focusing a little less on what we can actually see and measure is a good way to ensure the new addition.

Think about it…

---

*Lest you think Piotr had way too much time on his hands physicists study knots because they think that matter may be composed of string-like, possibly knotted, pieces of space time. Thus "String Theory." Interesting stuff—especially if you have a bottle of aspirin around.

CHAPTER 8

ABOUT GENERALS AND CEOS

Originally Published
December 2002

Sun Tzu said a great general (e.g. a great CEO) puts his army (employees) beyond the possibility of defeat. The general then waits, studying the enemy (your competition). When the general decides the enemy is "truly" weak he/she strikes decisively. "Truly" weak because a great general knows a skillful foe, another great general, may have his force appear strong, when they are actually weak—to keep their enemy away. And may appear weak when they are actually strong—in order to draw the enemy to them, generally into a trap on fatal ground of the general's own choosing.

Sun Tzu also said, "A great general (CEO) controls his enemy (competition)."

It is essential to understand that war and business are both about the same thing. They are about winning. Winning in the least amount of time, at the lowest possible cost and for the greatest reward possible."

Think about it...

CHAPTER 9

CONTROLLING NAPOLEON

*Originally Published
January 2003*

RULE: "The primary target of a great general (CEO) is the mind of the opposing general (CEO)."

I discuss elsewhere how, when facing a superior enemy (your competition) you should grab something they cherish to slow or stop them. Military history provides many examples of this, one being the final months of the Napoleonic Wars in 1814. Instead of hitting Napoleon head-on the Allies actually turned away from him and captured Paris instead. This demoralized the country and forced Napoleon to surrender. His ability to compete was effectively over.

Any general (CEO) knows a major goal of strategy is to diminish the enemy's ability to resist (e.g., to compete in the target marketplace). But a great general knows destruction can often be avoided. By moving quickly, invisibly, "marching swiftly to places he is not expected" he can distract and disorient his lesser opposition causing him to weaken or even abandon key points leading to their capture.

There are lots of ways to do this. Be creative, maybe a bit audacious. Ask yourself "How can I get in their way? What can I take that they need? Etc. As good recruiters we do it by removing a competitor's key executives. This last move can have devastating, long ranging results but the same rules apply to real estate, patents, court action, etc. One of the surest ways to get into your competitor's head is to reach out of nowhere and grab something of theirs. The question for you is simple: "What can I take?"

Think about it...

CHAPTER 10

AVOIDING YOUR OWN CHARGE OF THE LIGHT BRIGADE

Originally Published
December 2011

> *To paraphrase an ancient Greek writer:*
> *Ten good shoulders, wisely led,*
> *Will beat a hundred without a head.*
>
> *-Euripides*
>
> *"The famous Charge of the Light Brigade is a useful study because it broke so many classic rules of basic management. Inflated egos didn't help things either. "*
>
> *-Tal Newhart*

Let's look at the famous "Charge of the Light Brigade." It happened on October 25, 1854 during the Crimean War with the British fighting the Russians. The disaster happened for the same reason a lot of businesses fail: bad communication brought upon by a lethal collection of inflated egos.

In an act that appears to be of unfathomable stupidity the British Lieutenant-General the Earl of Cardigan ordered his light brigade (the "light" was because they were lightly armed, as opposed to the "heavy brigade") to attack the Russian artillery positions. Success was impossible. The charge was through a narrow valley a mile and a quarter long. Russian guns were at the end of the valley and gunners were on both sides, forming a classic death box. In fact, some of Cardigan's men did manage to get through to the guns, but were then surrounded by the Russian troops. When they turned to retreat they were easy targets. The whole thing took about 20 minutes and cost about a third of Cardigan's force. And of course there is the Tennyson poem to remind everybody about it forever (sort of like our modern social media…).

But what really went wrong, and why, it is vaguely familiar if you regularly read the Wall Street Journal.

As is often the case, there was a sequence of careless—and completely avoidable—mistakes. And they all came down to poor 'corpcraft' (see my definition of corpcraft elsewhere). A successful attack was clearly hopeless. That was obvious—as is almost always the case in war (and business), success or failure is decided before the battle. And again, as in business, after the "first stupid mistake" was made, management suddenly couldn't get anything right and the situation (and equity holder value) disintegrated with shocking speed.

In a nutshell this is the famous story of The Charge of the Light Brigade. It's amazing that generally intelligent commanders, which these gentlemen were, could make such foolish mistakes. But, just as in the corporate world, that happens. The real problem is that a single minor mistake can set off what around here we call a "negative cascade". (As opposed to a positive cascade which is what you and your equity holders want: good events leading to good events, etc.) A negative cascade is simple: think dominos. Big expensive ones.

But here's the detail and it is easy to compare this to something you've probably observed or personally experienced:

Lord Raglan, the English commander (a.k.a. the Boss here), looked across a broad landscape, and from his high vantage point on a hill, could see the enemy (the competition) in the distance trying to remove some captured English cannons. Since captured cannons were a metric of victory or defeat in a battle this was a Bad Thing. Raglan sent down another in a sequence of orders to Lieutenant-General the Earl of Lucan—who was in a position 600 feet lower in elevation and didn't have the same view—to recover the cannons "immediate" [sic]. The order was given to another officer's aide-de-camp, Captain Edward Nolan, for delivery—Captain Nolan was chosen because he was an accomplished horseman and would take a speedy, more direct route down to Lucan. He did this, probably loving it, because he was a known showoff.

So Nolan delivered the order to Lucan to attack and regain the cannons. Reading the order Lord Lucan was justifiably baffled and reasonably asked for clarification because he couldn't actually *see* any cannons. Nolan, eager to see some "real cavalry action", arrogantly waved his arm in the general direction of the Russian front and snapped "There, my Lord, is your enemy. There are your guns." Nolan repeated that the order was to attack immediately then trotted off to talk to another officer. Lord Lucan, flawed by pride, and always at odds with the arrogant Nolan (Nolan had authored books on cavalry tactics and made sure everybody knew it), failed to ask Nolan for further clarification. *Note: Like Lord Raglan, Captain Nolan had seen the location of the cannons that were obscured from Lucan's view because of the topography. But Nolan didn't accurately point to where the cannons were—he merely swept his arm across the landscape in the general direction of the Russians.* As you can see, the cascade now accelerates towards preventable disaster.

Lord Lucan rode over to the commander of the light brigade, the Earl of Cardigan (and his trusty horse Ronald). Lucan and Cardigan hated each other (Cardigan had been married to Lucan's youngest sister but was now separated from her) and, again, there was no useful discussion. Lucan simply ordered Cardigan to attack 'down the valley' with his light brigade. Cardigan pointed out the fact there were numerous enemy positions in the vicinity to which Lord Lucan simply replied Cardigan should take the ride at moderate speed so as not to exhaust the horses (good news for Ronald). Lucan would follow up with the heavy brigade. The cascade continues.

So off they rode into "The Valley of Death". Twenty minutes later it was over. Nolan died dramatically in the charge, ostensibly trying to ride forward to warn Cardigan he was headed in the wrong direction (some historians disagree with this interpretation—nobody argues he was the first to die). Lucan, seeing what was happening to the light brigade in front, turned the heavy brigade around uttering the famous line: "They shall not have the heavy."

The high level military history view says that the attack was a perfect misapplication of the sound strategy of applying superior force at a position of an enemy's weakness (e.g. your competition, also see the Southwest Airlines comments elsewhere in this collection).

But that's the easy way out. What happened was that the functional CEO (Lord Raglan) made a terrifically dumb mistake (the cannons were clearly lost to the

Russians). That mistake, foolish in itself, compounded itself through a sequence of unquestioning levels of management (accelerating the negative cascade). In the final analysis it was Cardigan who took the most heat because he led the actual charge straight into the cannon battery. Cardigan, of course, blamed Lucan. And Lucan, of course, blamed the dead Nolan for the vague delivery of the orders. Nothing's changed. This happens with poor management all the time. Look around. Hopefully you don't see it, but you probably do.

It all sounds uncomfortably familiar doesn't it? How many boards and executive committees behave the same way?

Let's take a look at this via a few very broad strokes:

1. Underestimation of a major obstacle. Raglan, like a lot of successful CEOs, probably thought "I've figured this out. Nothing's changed. Go get the cannons." Raglan had convinced himself he was the "master of the universe" and that he knew everything. Toss in a little of the "I can *do* anything" syndrome and it spells disaster. It's the same in the market place. In his mind Raglan saw only the cannons being recaptured. He failed to think of the process. Does the name Vivendi ring a bell (sorry Jean-Marie)?
2. Faced with a rapidly deteriorating situation Cardigan continued his charge. A Great CEO sometimes has to admit that he or she is wrong.

Sun Tzu said excess pride in a general is a bad thing (poor corpcraft) because they worry too much about what others think of them. Even smart CEOs sometimes continue to throw massive resources at projects (often pet projects) that can't work. Consider Ross Johnson of R.J. Reynolds and his so-called smokeless Premiere cigarettes. Like Cardigan, Ross continued the charge to prove "he could do it". It cost Ross a couple billion RJR dollars and Cardigan a couple hundred men. Great generals and great CEOs can admit that sometimes "you really can't get there from here". They can say it even though there's always somebody like Captain Nolan who will say "You see! I knew he couldn't do it!" Great leaders admit they made a mistake and move on, limiting the destruction. Good managers don't compound their errors. (See the chapter about mistakes.)

3. Another mistake Raglan made was his assumption of domination in a fluid state. Raglan thought he dominated the landscape (e.g., marketplace). But there were what amounted to "marketplace eddies" where he could be overpowered. Great generals and CEOs know that battlefield or market domination is a highly dynamic thing. They know that constant adjustment and tuning isn't optional, it's *required*.

4. Lord Lucan failed to get clarification from Captain Nolan and Nolan failed to pass on relevant information. A Great leader knows he or she has to listen to—*pursue, understand and act upon*—any credible source of information potentially relevant to the survival of the company. In many cases information "doesn't know where to go" in an enterprise. That's a serious flaw in a company since sometimes tiny pieces of information can lead to the destruction of even a huge company. The challenge is that extremely vital information frequently first presents itself in remote places along the outer edges of the organization. The datum or event may seem innocuous to the casual observer but can, if not acted upon decisively, cripple or even collapse a major enterprise. But that wasn't the case with the light brigade. Captain Nolan had the critical piece of information—he had seen the location of the cannons! But, in the heat of the moment he didn't pass it along. And Lucan didn't ask him to explain further because he felt Nolan was his inferior and Lucan himself would look bad or somehow weak by asking. Great leaders give, and get, the information needed. Lucan knew he had incomplete information but chose to act anyway. No greatness there. Just poor corpcraft.

So off they rode into "a mile long jaw of death."

The real tragedy here is how senseless it all was. The biggest box in the failure matrix was simply poor communication. The same thing frequently happens on Boards of Directors. Board level things often don't happen like they should because the board doesn't function as a proper, fluid team (and this has nothing to do with Sarbanes-Oxley, that's a downstream consideration).

Remember, in business the cannons are always there, somewhere. But there's no reason to ride into them.

Think about it...

My thanks to the British Government for their help in this account. –TN

CHAPTER 11

LUCIUS QUINCTIUS CINCINNATUS: THE PERFECT LEADER?

Originally Published
October 2003

As senior recruiters we are constantly studying the idea of "leadership". We need to understand it before we can reliably see it and identifying it is a large part of our job. We spend a lot of our time judging who really has it vs. "fractionals" or outright posers (resumes being one of the greatest outlets of fictional prose known to man…). But that's just the beginning. What's frustrating is that a good "leader" can still lead a company to destruction, especially if the board isn't strong. So, in our playbook, it goes beyond who can "lead", you have to know to where that person will tend to lead a company (or military force in that context). So it's complicated. Our company term "corpcraft" only begins to describe it.

However, you have to start somewhere and the past is always useful. Any serious student of leadership will tell you one of history's greatest leaders was Lucius Quinctius Cincinnatus. Even George Washington, clearly a great leader, partially modeled himself after Cincinnatus.

Here is the short and valuable story of Lucius Quinctius Cincinnatus.

In 458 BC Rome was in danger of falling to the Aequi and Voslcians, two nearby tribes. Roman law at the time had a provision to basically draft a "dictator" in times of great peril. Rome was then a republic and had no emperor. The dictator was given absolute power for a period of 6 months. Of course, during this time the potential for the dictator to abuse his power was on everybody's mind.

Due to the imminent threat to Rome the Senate knew they needed a real leader. The group (think Board of Directors) looked around itself and, not seeing the required talent, decided to draft Cincinnatus, a former Senate member who had resigned in disgrace over something his son had done (evidently children could be a problem even then...). *This is key:* The members of the Senate knew that under similar circumstances none of them would have stepped down. They knew they needed somebody of strong character.

The delegation found Cincinnatus at his farm. Note: The farm was the smallest size plot that would allow for Roman citizenship. Cincinnatus was literally behind a plow working the field when they arrived. The delegation handed him some papers and saluted him as dictator. Cincinnatus donned a toga and they all went back to Rome. Pretty straightforward.

In a short time Cincinnatus had taken over command of the army, then marched out to meet and quickly defeat the Aequi and Voslcians. He returned to Rome a hero.

But what did he do then? Rather than hang around and abuse his unlimited power he resigned and went back to plow his fields and tend to his family. The whole thing took 15 days. Wow.

It's easy to see why history points to Cincinnatus as a great leader. He was a leader in the purist sense. He did what was asked; lead Rome to a solution without regard for personal gain. And then, his job done, he simply went home.

Similarly, history sometimes refers to George Washington as "the American Cincinnatus". Washington too did great things then went back to his farm. He just coolly delivered what he was asked to do. That's a great trait for great CEOs.

Think about it…

And yes, the city of Cincinnati was named after Lucius Quinctius Cincinnatus.

CHAPTER 12

A CEO TALKS ABOUT THE IMPORTANCE OF GROKKING

***Originally Published
December 2011***

I had lunch last week with an author of two once bestselling business books. I was interviewing him on behalf of a client for a consulting job. I was brought in because the client wanted a good arm's length interview they could easily pass around the C-suite. The writer had once run a very large corporation, did so famously, and wrote well about it. The recorded interview itself was telling and useful relative to the client's decision about whether or not to consider him further for the assignment. But it was the informal discussion later when he brought up a useful notion he said I could share with other Corpwar readers.

This notion is his very deep seated belief of something called "grokking". This was what he always looked for in his inner team members. He said it was an even denser form of value, to him, than what I call a "corporate warrior" (a phrase he considers a bit pop and superficial). I had never heard the term "grok" before so I asked what it meant to him in a functional, as well as philosophical, sense.

He answered, "It means the guy or gal is really inside the skill set of something. It's not an external layer. Most people with good skills wear them like good clothes. But it's still external. A layer on the outside. A person that groks something knows it so thoroughly it has become part of them. It has become their retina through which they see everything."

"Doesn't that singular focus lead to a kind of social dysfunction?" I asked having seen exactly that in software engineers, actuaries, etc., that I have been responsible for hiring.

"Sometimes. Those guys we just put into a nice corner with good tools and keep the place dusted for them. Everybody that's properly employed adds equity holder value in their own way; if they grok something of value to the organization, and therefore the equity holder, then that value add is pretty high. You need to support it and use it. My ongoing goal, perfection really, is having our most important critical paths composed of these kinds of people doing what they grok. It's a beautiful thing to watch projects flash up those human chains once they are assembled."

I asked him what he grokked. He smiled and said "Well, that's simple. People."

I left the meeting asking myself what I "grok" in my professional life, if indeed anything. I concluded it would be recruiting in its various flavors, such as doing useful interviews and selling exceptional candidates that don't want to move jobs; that it will improve their life in various meaningful ways to take that leap. It's a fairly diverse skill cloud that, when brought to a singular focus, is actually somewhat limited, which I found humbling.

It might be beneficial to ask yourself the same question: "Do I grok at anything, and if so what?" After looking at your core team members with the same question in mind, suggest they do the same. And so on. It's a useful exercise for accelerating things.

Think about it...

CHAPTER 13

A READER'S STRATEGY—ACT LIKE A SNAKE

***Originally Published
February 2003***

Last week we received an insightful e-mail from the famous CEO of a Fortune 100 company. He asked a quick technical question about e-mail and the use of our term 'corpcraft'. As a postscript to our answer we asked him how he did it—how he had managed to consistently add or protect so much equity holder value, even in this grim market. His answer was illustrative given his fame as a fierce competitor, in both his business and personal life.

"Tal, to put it in terms you would appreciate: I learned a long time ago to act like a shuai-jan, you know, the snake. That and not being worried about personal embarrassment which opens up a lot of possibilities my counterparts avoid."

For the non-herpetologists out there: a shuai-jan is a snake mentioned in ancient Chinese texts on battle tactics: *"When you attack the shuai-jan's head, it attacks you with its tail. When you strike its tail it attacks with his head. Strike at its middle and both ends will attack you."*

Both traits help explain his happy equity holders.

Think about it...

CHAPTER 14

GETTING AHEAD THROUGH FAKERY

Originally Published
May 2003

> *"Make an uproar in the east, but attack in the west,"*
>
> -Sun Tzu, 500 B.C.

What is being illustrated below—aside from considerable hubris—are the timeless battle principles of deception and control. They can work great in business too. Your competitive intelligence says your competition is going to make an active, perhaps aggressive move. That's fine, but YOU must control their actions—and they must not know you are doing that. As always, a great CEO, just like a great general, controls the movements of his competition, often by creative and cost-effective fakery. Below a Fortune-level Chairman/CEO comments on how he does it...

In reaction to the "snake comment" of a few months ago, where the CEO compared himself to a Chinese snake (to date, about 110 readers have properly guessed who the CEO is), one comment that is consistent and certainly reflects good corpcraft follows:

"I would never attack like a snake. That guy's crazy. All that thrashing around? Even with the best management in the world it's too difficult to control. It's better to be subtle. [For example] we send out inexpensive teams just to show up, make some noise, look interested, then disappear. The next thing you know they've [the competition] sent in their own people and have started spending money to get in front of us because we're supposed to be so smart. Fact is we're leading them all around by their corporate nose ring and they don't even know it. It's interesting that they haven't figured it out. But it's great for our equity holders, and pretty bad for theirs."

When asked about the chance that his competition have, in fact, 'figured it out' he responded, with a grin: "Impossible. I have much better spies!"

I love this guy. He gets it.

Here, getting his competition to open up resource draining outlets, where the CEO has no intention of competing, allows him to focus his best resources, all initially deployed in secret, on opening locations where he gets a very solid market jump on those that can still follow. Note: The individual stock performance of these competing companies comes as no surprise.

So think about it: What illusion can you create to get your competition to do something they really shouldn't…

CHAPTER 15

HOW TO AVOID YOUR OWN WATERLOO

**Originally Published
January 2004**

> *"A conqueror is like a cannonball...he can only move forward. Once he rebounds his career is over."*
>
> -The victorious Duke of Wellington in the wake of Waterloo when asked why Napoleon chose to attack, rather than simply defend, France after escaping from his exile on Elba.

What happened to Napoleon Bonaparte at the Battle of Waterloo is a useful illustration of how a brilliant strategist can make disastrous, career terminating mistakes. But rather than focus on the minutia of the convoluted battle it's more useful here to look at the broader mistakes he made as a manager. Why? Because, unfortunately, we see these mistakes all too frequently in business leaders. Do you see anything familiar in the summary below?

A brief history

In 1799, driven by his dream of making France a European empire, Napoleon Bonaparte, a highly talented and experienced military leader, carried out a coup against the Directory (First Republic of France) and eventually made himself Emperor. This strategy worked and in 1802 the Republic of France was recognized with the Peace of Amiens.

You would think this would be enough. But no, because Napoleon was a megalomaniac (like some CEOs we all know—Donald, are you still reading?), this was insufficient. He wanted France to be the most powerful country (business!) in Europe. So in 1803, he declared war on his neighboring countries plus Britain. This was the beginning of the Napoleonic Wars which went on between France and the Allies for 11 years. The Allies finally defeated France in 1814 forcing Napoleon to abdicate at the Treaty of Fontainebleau. He was exiled to the pleasant island of Elba off the coast of Italy. Elba is part of Tuscany, and Tuscany is wonderful. He was even given the title Emperor of

Elba and rule over its 100,000 people. Not bad. But not enough either.

He stuck it out for 11 months then escaped on March 1st of 1815 with a contingent of 1,000 men. He reached Paris on March 20th and thus began the "100 Days Campaign". Horrified at his return from exile the Allies who, unfortunately for Napoleon, happened to be meeting in Vienna at the time discussing the territorial balance in Europe, immediately declared war on him. To understand the instant resolve to get rid of the fellow it's useful to remember Napoleon was a Very Bad Man (an "Evil Doer!") and was thought, by some, to be a sort of Hitler or Saddam of his day. He wanted to conquer Europe and everybody knew it. This is why a large coalition of forces could easily be formed to deal with him in a completely unambiguous manner. It would be like combining two very large computer manufacturers to give Dell and IBM a hard time...

So it was France/Napoleon against: the British, Dutch, Belgian, Russian, Prussian and Austrian armies. The Anglo-Dutch force was commanded by the cool, aristocratic Irishman Arthur Wellesley (a.k.a. the Duke of Wellington) with Field-Marshal Gebhard Leberecht von Blücher commanding the Prussians. Both Wellington and Blücher had experience against Napoleon and Blücher was the only person to beat Napoleon more than once. So Wellington and Blücher understood their opponent. Blücher, especially, hated Napoleon and since Blücher was entering old age he had little to fear from Bonaparte—and competing against an opponent that has no fear (and this includes business leaders) is always dangerous. Even so, Napoleon thought neither Wellington nor Blücher were "worthy" opponents.

Napoleon's goal was to use the classic battle tactic of the Central Position which he was expert in. This is how a small force (a small business) can defeat a bigger one. While he was seriously outnumbered with his 125,000 men, this was only the case if the two opposing forces (Wellington with 110,000 men and Blücher with 120,000) were able to combine. It was extremely important that Napoleon prevent this from happening—he had to get between them (gain the "central position") and fight them in series since he knew victory was almost impossible against the combined force. If he took them on separately he could succeed.

Since he moved so quickly toward Belgium, Napoleon knew a fleeting set of circumstances was in his favor—the Allies were still moving towards each other. To exploit this Napoleon ordered a young Marshal Ney to take 24,000 men and attack part of Wellington's forces at Quatre Bras. Napoleon took the remaining force and attacked the approaching Prussian forces under Blücher at the town of Ligny.

Napoleon shattered the Prussians and almost killed Blücher. Unfortunately, ego driven Napoleon made a critical competitive mistake—as they started retreating he concluded Blücher was beaten and out of the fight, thus preventing him from aiding Wellington.

The young Lt. Ney was also making a critical mistake. Rather than taking the initiative, he waited for clarifying communications from Napoleon before attacking the Dutch force led by the disastrously inexperienced Prince of Orange (the son of the King of the Netherlands). When Ney finally attacked he sent much of the Dutch force fleeing but the critical pause allowed time for Wellington's main battle force to arrive and attack which in turn seriously weakened Ney's numbers. However, it wasn't a draw—Wellington retreated only a few kilometers north. Had Ney been more aggressive he could have done far more damage, which would have been useful later. In fact, some military historians believe Ney's performance at Quatre Bras was elemental in Napoleon's defeat later.

However, so far, so good. Napoleon had managed to keep the two allied forces from combining and inflicted serious damage while doing so. On the surface it was an utterly brilliant victory for the pugnacious Frenchman.

Unfortunately it was short lived. The next day, June 18th, Napoleon was likely to regret leaving lovely Elba.

The decisive battle was at Waterloo, about 11 miles from Brussels. The day started with a torrential downpour. This made it extremely difficult for Napoleon to move his artillery even with a dozen horses and 15 men pulling on each cannon. This was a critical problem as it delayed the battle allowing Blücher's reorganized army time to move closer. Realizing this Napoleon had dispatched almost a third of his force under Marshal Grouchy to march north and engage Blücher to prevent him from entering the main fight. Had Grouchy been successful things might have been different. But Grouchy had no real depth as a leader and blew the assignment badly. Napoleon was paying the price for his hasty staffing decisions (We've all been there, right?). At 11:30 that morning Bonaparte gave the order to start the general attack and with it 100 cannons let loose.

The battle lasted the rest of the day and into the night. Unfortunately for Napoleon, Grouchy never reached Blücher's main force. This raised many questions. There's a saying in war: "Follow the noise to find the battle." It was obvious where the battle was being waged because of the massive sound of all the cannons (And, if you don't already know, cannons are LOUD!). But Grouchy, under nominal orders to prevent Blücher from moving toward Napoleon, didn't join the main battle but chose rather to engage Blücher's tenacious rearguard around the town of Wavre; this provided Grouchy a minor, and basically meaningless, victory. Had Grouchy had more initiative and brought his 30,000 fresh men into the main fight Napoleon might well have won at Waterloo. As it was, Grouchy's actions allowed the Prussians to merge with Wellington's now weakened forces. Napoleon's central position had collapsed (the manpower math was all wrong). When this happened Napoleon was doomed.

But, he fought on. It was only with the arrival of Blücher's force, suddenly combining with the British, that the French turned and fled "for their lives". It was 9:30 that night that Blücher and Wellington embraced each other in success. Four days later in Paris Napoleon abdicated a second time and was sent off to the windswept island of St. Helena in the middle of the South Atlantic where he died five and a half years later. Unlike the bucolic Elba, St. Helena was no picnic spot.

History puts the blame for the disaster of Waterloo on Napoleon because he was the leader. And that's certainly as it should be. He was the CEO. That said, sure, he made a lot of mistakes (see the summary list below) but frankly I think he had some serious staffing issues in the form of Ney and Grouchy. Had they been up to the tasks Napoleon assigned to them, the outcome would likely have been different and the face of Europe changed for many years to come.

Little known fact: The "Battle of Waterloo" isn't named for where the fighting took place. Although that's where most of the battle happened, it's called that because that is where the Duke of Wellington spent the night before the battle and it was his own tradition to name the battle after where he slept prior to a victorious battle. So perhaps there was more than one big ego involved…

Here is a summary of Napoleon's management traits and the mistakes resulting in The Battle of Waterloo (a.k.a. CEO traits and actions of questionable value…)

1. Impossibly arrogant and egotistical leading to:
   a. Careless rush to action thinking he could do no wrong
   b. Ignored the opinions of others
   c. Disrespected the competition (thought Wellington and Blücher were not "worthy" even though they had previously beaten him)
   d. Relied on his previously successful tactics, closing his mind to new ideas (victim of his previous success)
2. Underestimated the sheer conviction of the competition
3. Rushed selection of incompetent senior management (Ney and Grouchy)
4. Poor lines of communication with divisional management
5. Made the fundamental mistake of choosing the wrong goal and bet the company on it…and lost

Very basic stuff, really.

Think about it…

CHAPTER 16

WHAT WE SEEM TO BE FORGETTING & WHY WE'RE IN TROUBLE

**Originally Published
October 2008**

AKA: If your head's comfortably in the sand, just fire yourself.

A finance journalist, and reader of this occasional newsletter, called last week to ask what I thought about the $700 billion bailout plan. The conversation quickly expanded into a discussion of, "What happened?" He was referring to the larger picture, as in "What happened to us (the United States)?" Basically, he was asking what happened to Chrysler, Wall Street, Main Street, you and me, etc. In fact, as I write this on Monday the Dow is down 400 (four h-u-n-d-r-e-d) points.

Well obviously, it's complex. But I think a lot of it stems from 9/11 which was so classic it now seems grimly inevitable. I wrote about the tactic in a corporate setting in a Corpwar way back in 2003. Al-Zawahiri, one of Osama bin Laden's key strategists, knew the only way to bring us down, arguably the most "powerful" civilization in history, *was to help us bring ourselves down*. Aside from our spirit, America is also a business and as such we "behave" like a business. And all businesses have their weaknesses which are too often discernable to our competition (e.g. al-Zawahiri, or picture your own competition—there really is no difference). So al-Zawahiri helped come up with this cheap little plan, pretty crude really, and sent a huge arrow dead center into our economic heart. And, let's face it, it's been pretty rough sailing ever since. And if you don't think so, you and I don't live on the same planet.

If you think your business is any different you are part of the problem. You need to think better. You need to think stronger. We all work for our stakeholders. We OWE them our best, now more than ever, because things are starting to fall apart. And if we don't give them our best we should be replaced. Period. This is no time for dull, obtuse, thinking folks.

I've taken on the role of new business development for a candidate interviewing company (technically a spin-off) and have noticed a couple of alarming things. To put this in context the service does screening interviews of a client's "short list" of an open job's candidates and makes those recordings available to the hiring group so they can efficiently comment on whether or not they think a candidate would be a good fit to the position, the team, the company, etc. Pretty simple.

Now, managers that use the service typically love it because of the time savings but, conversely, some really hate it (actually loathe everything about it). When I drill in to understand why, it's usually because "things work well enough as they are". All I can say is, *"Stop right there."* This is the kind of thinking that some clever guy in a corporate cave somewhere (a.k.a. your competition, some of whom you probably aren't even aware of) is waiting to exploit. This mindset insists "things are cool enough now, we'll survive". Really? Think again. If you're sitting around thinking your business is some sort of invincible fort I GUARANTEE you somebody, somewhere, is x-raying your walls to find weak spots. They are focusing on YOU, trying to find YOUR Twin Towers. And we all know the potential result.

Another thing I've noticed because of the interviewing service is the quality of many of the candidates (the resumes are supplied by the client's HR department, or retained recruiting companies, and we have no control over what we get). I do some of the interviews myself and listen to many of the others and I'm often shocked at what I hear. We typically interview 4-5 candidates per position and often 1 or 2, sometimes even 3 of these candidates are pretty poorly qualified for the position (even internal candidates up for internal transfer or a succession move). Sometimes egregiously so. It's just so vivid in the recording that they can't do the job you have to ask yourself, how did these people get on the short list? Sometimes, of course, our interviewing process lets somebody really shine that looks weak on paper (that's great when it happens, by the way), but more often we uncover expensive hiring mistakes waiting to happen. Often their only real skill is knowing how to game the hiring system. Thank god people like us help weed them out.

Look, you need to impress everybody around you, everybody in your company, that there are barbarians at the corporate gate, because functionally there really are. This is no time for lazy, yesterday thinking because competitors that need to eat are hunkered down trying to figure out how to steal your food.

This is capitalism folks. Your competition doesn't care if you starve to death.

Think hard about it…

CHAPTER 17

THE KEY TRAIT OF A TRUE CORPORATE WARRIOR

Originally Published
August 2010

Plus, if and when it's ok for a CEO to lie.
Part I

A discussion on an Atlantic Flight

It was a busy summer filling several finance and ops positions along the East Coast and in Europe. On a trip home to Chicago from candidate interviews in Zurich and Brussels I couldn't help but notice the distinguished passenger beside me (Kiton suit, low key Audemars Piguet watch, posture, etc.). Trying not to stare, I finally recognized him as a heavy speaker at the World Economic Forum in Davos last winter. A while after takeoff he looked over at my printed legal pad which has Business is Warfare printed across the top in bold letters. He casually asked me about it and I mentioned I do this occasional newsletter. He then said he was, in fact, a longtime reader (e.g. back to 2002!). He said its usefulness was "inconsistent" but on occasion liked sending it along to his staff as well as his son who, he added in a quiet, disappointed tone, "utterly lacks the required edge to change things." He stared past me out the window as he said it. His tired expression said he had concluded the family greatness was going to end with himself. The son wasn't interested in carrying the torch and, in fact, would only drop it repeatedly if he tried. I guess that makes most dads sad. He settled back into his seat and read the FT.

After about an hour of silence and a couple more drinks he looked over and held up his left forefinger. "Tell me the one trait that you look hardest for."

"In what?" I asked looking up from my pad.

"In one of your 'corporate warriors'. What's the proof at the core? When I invest in companies I look for a lot of things but focus on the real cash flows. What do you look for?"

This had become so intuitive for me I had to think about how to put it. He stepped in, "Ok, start with the lowest common denominator."

"Well, that's simple. Expertise."

"That's too simplistic."

"But the client needs it," I said. "How else does the employee pay his way?"

"To do what?"

"Drive value to the business' ownership," I answered.

"You think all it takes is expertise? That's nothing. Every executive has that, otherwise they shouldn't even have the job."

"But it happens. It happens all the time."

"Of course. And when no one does something about it companies wither. What else?"

"Relevant experience."

He rolled his eyes. "Obviously. What else?"

"Ok. Demonstrated loyalty."

He smiled. "I somehow knew that would be on your list."

"Why?"

"You really do have a sort of platoon mentality, don't you." he said. "So loyalty would be important to you. But let me ask you this, loyalty to whom? The idea? The team? The boss? Themselves? Society?"

Suddenly I needed something really stiff to drink. I was outgunned and I knew it. He knew it too. He was my Professor Kingsfield all over again. I didn't know whether to fold and go back to work on my speech or to maneuver. I paused then came back with: "All those but mostly to the stakeholders."

Wherever he was driving this caused a bend in his road. "The stakeholders?" he asked.

"If the employee takes a paycheck, of course. That's who they work for. Everything has to eventually point to maximizing the owners' enrichment."

"But what do the equity holders know?"

"Who cares? That's not the point," I answered flatly.

"What about honor?"

"Well, it's always better to behave so you don't have to apologize."

"Apologize?" he asked.

"It's part of any job, especially a senior one, to have to make tough choices. Honor dictates you make them for the right reasons. I think it's part of loyalty."

"Don't you find that these days loyalty has become too portable?" he asked.

"Perhaps. But as long as somebody is taking a paycheck they have to earn it. And a good executive, corporate warrior or otherwise, will persevere until the moment they move on. That too is part of honor, at least as I see it."

"Interesting. But you still haven't told me what's in the center of this 'loyal, honorable expert warrior with useful experience.' These are just ornaments on the tree. What's the trunk made of?"

"Simple. They have to be driven to win. Otherwise, there's no real movement, just vibration."

He thought about this for several seconds then smiled and reached into his coat. He pulled out a business card and reached over, setting it on my pad. "I guess that just about says it."

I examined the engraved card then looked over at him. "Thank you. Now, tell me about your son."

Part II

About an hour later we were in the thick of another discussion. It had spun out of the notion of honor and the lengths to which senior managers should go to win for their equity holders and how much emphasis should be placed on social good. We had entered into the sticky subject of management lying.

"No, a CEO should never lie," he said flatly. "That's taking it too far. Look at Enron," the famous manager said.

I set my drink down and looked over. "Nice, but unfortunately business has gotten to the point that natural selection favors the deceitful."

"And you help."

I frowned. "I resent that. You make it sound like I push for deceit for deceit's sake. That's not true. That would be stupid and shortsighted."

"Sure you do. I've probably suffered through every column you've written for 5 years. Most of them center around some creative form of deception in the 'corporate battlefield' as you unflaggingly put it."

"And that's wrong? How can that be wrong? Don't equity holders have a right to expect their CEOs and managers to do what's necessary to create sustainable increases in equity holder value? Note the emphasis on 'sustainable'."

"Of course. But I don't believe that has to include institutionalized lying," he said, then paused to sip his scotch.

I leaned back into my seat. This wasn't going well. I looked over, "Ok, what about a 'noble lie'? A lie told as a substitute for violence and to prevent harm. Would you lie to a mugger to protect your son from a beating? Is that lie ok?"

"Of course, because you've done a good thing and there are no social consequences," he answered confidently.

"Well, in a strict sense, yes there are. Just ask the potential beater—you efficiently modified his ability to make an accurate decision by lying to him. Therein lays the power of deceit. It alters perceived reality so different decisions are made. Informed decisions, but with bad information. So don't tell me you haven't damaged social trust because you have. But in those circumstances it's ok. Right?"

I glanced into his hooded eyes as he watched and listened. It was one of those moments when you realize most people in a conversation just wait for you to stop making noise so they can say something. But that wasn't the case here. I was confident in what I was saying but the intensity of his listening was both welcome and yet unnerving. Plus, there seemed to be something else going on. A kind of weird weight hung in the cabin air between us.

I continued, "Well, then. So it's ok to lie as long as you're defending something from harm. You've used a lie to coerce and modify behavior, so it's no different than a club; they're both coercive weapons. And weapons make people do things they don't want to do."

There was another long, heavy pause between us.

He finally said, "You're going to sit there and seriously tell me it's ok for a corporate officer to lie? You preach about the sustainability of profits, but you can't reliably sustain profits that are based on lies because lies themselves are unsustainable. "

"No, I'm saying it depends. Lying isn't just a tool for managers that lack the skill to come up with a truthful alternative. Those lies are unsupportable. But there are times when deception should be given technical consideration just as you would any potentially useful tool."

"Such as?"

"How about lying in war?" I asked.

"That's different. That isn't the world most people live in. In war things are different."

"How about corporate war?"

"Oh, here we go," he said with a depreciating tone.

"That's right. Here we go," I said, getting a little hot, but wary of jumping on my usual soapbox. "Does your competition lie about you, even in small ways, to get your customers?"

"Of course."

"And taking your customers hurts you?"

"Typically, of course."

"Ok, let's look at this," I said sharpening focus. "Your competition deploys deceit as a tool to hurt you. That's a pretty good definition of an enemy. And enemies, in my galaxy anyway, lose the right to be treated fairly."

"So in this sacred galaxy of yours you get to treat 'bad people' badly?"

"I get to treat them as they treat me. I was raised on the Golden Rule and experience has taught me it's a pretty good one."

"So once you have somehow divined someone is an enemy, then your moral compass loosens up a bit. Your acceptable tool-set becomes a bit 'broader'".

"Exactly," I said, hoping we were done.

He sat there for almost a minute before he spoke. "Your playbook has always intrigued me. On the surface it appears rational, then when you look closer it gets a bit twisted. Then it begins to make sense again. Unfortunately I'm not sure that's where it ends."

I couldn't tell if he was giving me a compliment. Probably not. I stared out the window at the cloudless ocean of blue and waited. I wanted to be out there somewhere flying my plane.

He went on, "As you view it, in times of competitor induced corporate war wouldn't a good CEO, a good corporate general, endeavor to make the competition, the enemy, seem even worse than they actually are in order to justify treating them even worse? By your rules, even though that is escalated deceit that would be characteristic of a better CEO than one that wouldn't do it. Right?"

It took a few seconds to get my arms around this. "Yes, because short wars are better than long ones. That's a Sun Tzuism that's pretty hard to argue with. Once you've been pulled into the ring, hit harder and end it quickly. That's a CEO's job as a leader and caretaker of his employees."

"But Tal, what about if a competitor hasn't shown themselves to be an enemy—they are playing by the rules. However, your CEO's experience dictates that it's just a ruse and they will become an enemy eventually. Your playbook seems to suggest it's ok to treat them like they MAY behave?"

"You're talking about preemptive behavior?" I asked. He nodded.

I smiled, "No, I think that's called prudent paranoia. In any case an entity has to behave in a way that is unambiguously hostile to be labeled an enemy. That said, it's only intelligent to 'hope for the best while planning for the worst'. Your equity holders expect that of you. And any good manager expects that from their crew. That's just good management. It's what they get paid to do."

"Ok, Tal, here's my take. The fact is most corporate deceit goes on internally within the [org] chart. The challenge is that lying is so expedient. And everybody wants more of what they want. The real issues are the trailing effects. You can never tell one lie because more are needed to shore up the one you told."

"I know. My father once told me lies, like money, compound. Just not in a good way," I said.

"I have found that managers that always tell the truth move up quicker and get more done simply because the truth is free standing; the truth doesn't require maintenance. Truthful managers simply have more time to think about improving themselves and the business. Unfortunately the rewards to a lie are typically immediate and obvious."

I thought about this a moment. "Of course. That's why people do it in the first place. People only lie for the reward. If there were no reward of some sort we wouldn't do it. Simple economics. Too bad the rewards for honesty are, by comparison, so diffuse. And diffuse rewards are often invisible to very bottom-line oriented management."

"No surprise," he said. "A solid bottom line is, after all, measured in dollars, not the philosophical warmth of having integrity. Sure, it counts, but it's hard to quantify. Numbers are easy."

"Exactly. And that's a problem. It is, however, the way it is," I said.

"Tal, the key for your so-called corporate warrior, the CEO slash general, is to incent honesty and thoroughness. He or she has to create a culture of creative, thorough thinking, where alternatives to deceit are rewarded. You can almost always find a truthful alternative. I learned a long time ago any rung on the org chart almost always emulates the rows above them. The youngsters copying the parents—so the parents have to be getting it right. Lazy workers lie, or at least they lie more and they have to be weeded out. And if an externally directed deception has to happen, really has to happen, and by that I mean there's no truthful alternative, then do it well. I liked your bit on FUD [Fear, Uncertainty and Doubt], by the way. That was useful."

I thought about this a moment. "Wait a minute. Just a few minutes ago you were saying a manager should never lie."

He smiled. "I know. Sorry about that."

"You mean you…lied?"

"Yes. But a 'noble lie'," he said relaxing into his chair. "I was protecting myself from a boring flight."

I reclined my seat and stared up at the ceiling. It was time to take my own advice; short wars are better than long ones. LOL.

Think about it…

CHAPTER 18

"THE FEINT": GENGHIS KHAN AND HENRY KRAVIS—DIFFERENT TIME, SAME TACTIC

*Originally Published
September 2007*

Rule: "A great general (CEO) controls the movements of his competition."

The Mongols under the rule of the brilliant Genghis Khan, perfected the feint, or feigned retreat, which had been in use for over a thousand years. It's deceptively simple but requires exacting execution (e.g. good management, a loyal team, signaling skills, etc.). If the enemy couldn't be shattered on the initial attack the Mongols had a special unit called the mangudai. The mangudai would first make a fearsome charge against the enemy and then would appear to flee in retreat. This was the feint. Thinking an easy victory was available the enemy would often pursue at speed. Not...good.

What they didn't know was they were, in fact, being controlled by the Mongol leaders (called orloks). The rest is as grim as it is obvious. As the opportunistic enemy chased the light and fast mangudai, hidden Mongol archers would start picking off the pursuers. When the calculated chaos ensued the heavy Mongol cavalry would swoop in and finish the job.

Henry Kravis did the same thing in one critical stage of his eventually successful bid for RJR Nabisco. His feint was when he went off skiing to Vail during the heat of the bidding. His competition in the deal, Peter Cohen et al., thought Kravis had given up and made the decisions based on that. Because of this *Henry essentially controlled the crucial next round of bids*, as in keeping them low, via his presumed retirement from the action. He then sprang his trap: At a crucial moment he showed up with a bid much higher than anyone else's. This threw the process into chaos which Kravis and Roberts skillfully, and successfully, exploited.

Ask yourself, does a competitor's move look too good to be true? Does their move appear to somehow benefit you? If so, question your next logical step as it could be straight into a classic controlling feint which is really nothing more than a simple snare. And a snare works only if someone is foolish enough to step into it. Don't let that someone be you.

Think about it…

CHAPTER 19

HOW A FAMOUS CEO STAYS SO CALM

Originally Published
March 2011

Hint: "The open folders will kill you."

Somewhere along the line I picked up the rule that says when you're having lunch with someone on their private jet you should pay special attention to what they have to say. Last week was such an occasion and I'd like to pass along part of the conversation. If you occasionally feel stressed out and overwhelmed you might find it useful.

As is our practice when we do an executive search we typically supply some video, or recorded audio, of the top candidates. Seeing, or hearing, the candidates, provides a better idea of who they really are. So it saves a lot of time, money and reduces hiring risk for the client. Normally we put all this material securely on the web so the hiring team can peruse it at their convenience. This saves even more time. It's a slick system and although low-tech by today's standards, works very well.

However, recently a client, a Fortune-level CEO and a way-back reader of this occasional newsletter (we've mentioned him previously), called up and asked me to bring the interview content over to Chicago Executive Airport (a busy corporate airport north of Chicago) and we'd go over the candidates for a senior finance position and then have some lunch.

We met on his Gulfstream (nice ride). After reviewing the video and resumes, and making some decisions, we put the work aside as the flight steward set the table for lunch which was brought over by a famous North Shore restaurant. I replied a cautious "Sure," to the host's comment: "I hope you like Atkins." For the curious the meal consisted of grilled tuna steak with a portabella, gorgonzola salad and a glass of One.6 Chardonnay (a "low carb" wine). For the record, I would have that meal again anytime, anywhere.

During lunch (which permanently altered my notion of "diet food") I noticed my host seemed totally relaxed and without distraction. This was notable to me because you almost never see it. Most people, from the McDonald's drive-thru window person, to Donald Trump (ok, maybe a bad example), have so much on their minds that you just know they aren't all there. And they know it themselves. But here was my host, a nationally important man responsible for over 50,000 employees, and ultimately responsible for countless projects and equity holders, and yet he had a relaxed "lightness" about him that suggested he had arrived someplace that I, and perhaps you too, want to be. So I asked him how he did it. Here is the salient part of the conversation almost verbatim:

He smiled at the initial question. "Ah, maybe it's just a trick. Maybe I'm as overwhelmed as the fella that brought the food. I just don't show it. Maybe it's a ruse."

Sipping the wine, I thought about this. "No. I don't think so. I'd be able to tell because that's my job and I'm good at it."

He smiled. "OK, then describe to me in a single word what you think you're observing, either by its presence or absence. Go ahead. You're creative, Tal. Give it a try."

I thought about this, then said, simply, "Carefree." I then looked around the luxurious $40 million jet and added, "Which strikes me as impossible!"

"Well, you're right. I absolutely am not carefree in the usual sense, but I am in a very important way."

Now we were getting somewhere. "And what way is that?"

"My mind is clear. And relaxed," he said, eating the crisp tuna. He then reached into his breast pocket, pulled out a dime store notepad, made a note on it with a nice fountain pen and replaced both in his pocket. The motion was fluid and seemed to take only a few seconds. I realized he'd done it a half dozen times since I arrived but this was the first time I really noticed. His motion was that practiced. That routine. Clearly he had done it thousands of times.

"So's mine," I announced confidently, referring to my mental state.

"But it's not," he said, waving his fork. "And, Tal, that's not a bad thing. It's just inefficient. Like most people you over and under react to situations, which means the situations control you. I've seen you do it. You need to remind yourself to respond appropriately."

I replied, "Like the old notion of reacting like water when you toss a pebble into it?"

"Exactly," he said smiling. "We're talking about the same thing. The water doesn't over or under react. It reacts appropriately. If you over or under react the input is controlling you. Phone calls. Meetings. E-mails and texts. I learned a long time ago to give everything exactly what it deserves. Nothing more. Nothing less. At the time I came to that understanding, it was a big step for me." As he said this the pad came out and a few seconds later glided back into his shirt pocket. Smoothly, like relaxed breathing. It was elegant.

In the background a Learjet roared down the runway and off toward the East. I confess to wondering if its expensive occupants were under or over reacting to something. I half expected my host to read my mind and whisper, "Over." I continued with my lunch. It was genuinely delicious.

There was an easy silence in the cabin. I finally asked, "I can understand the efficiency of a measured response. But that doesn't explain your notion of the clear and relaxed mind. You have to have more going on in your head than most anyone I know. How can you honestly say it's clear and relaxed?"

"Simple. No open folders," he said, pointing his fork towards his head. "The open folders can kill you."

"Excuse me? Open folders?"

"We all make commitments—far more than we are aware of, most of them to ourselves. The key is the way our subconscious mind handles them. Basically, all our outstanding commitments are kept track of. I think of these as open folders because literally that's what they are. Something unfinished and waiting for something. Waiting for action and closure."

"What's an example?"

"Anything you think of that you want to come back to. Think about the enormity of that. It's any task you need to do, *anything* you want to follow-up on. The moment you think of it, if you don't execute it right then, it becomes an open folder. Something that needs to happen in the future. The problem is, in a typical human being, the open folders sort of float around in your short term memory which is a finite space. In the majority of people it's very cluttered which is the opposite of having a clear mind."

"And the clutter creates stress?" I asked, reaching for the glass of peculiar, but tasty, wine.

"Of course. Because you've identified a responsibility you have, some task you need to do and your subconscious mind won't let you really relax until it's done. So you have to handle it. The problem is much of the time we "forget" it—but in reality, Tal, it's not gone. It's still up there. Still an open folder sponging up resources. After a while there's no more room so we get tense, lose focus, and become less effective. We founder."

Then it dawned on me. "Thus, the pad?"

"Thus the pad," he said, pulling it out and fanning it like a deck of playing cards. "This is where everything goes. And I mean absolutely everything. The key is you have to trust it. I know if I write it down it will resurface. [Note: This was later clarified. The little note pages, which are all dated, (idea, reference, action or desired outcome notations), are faxed to an admin support person for handling. The circle back/follow-up process is apparently quite rigid.] The point is I can then forget about it. Writing it down "closes the folder" freeing up bandwidth to think about something else."

"And what is that, typically?"

"Actually, a lot about family and other pleasant pastimes. But if it's business related, after envisioning a project's desired outcome, it's mostly next step related thinking. Much less big picture than you would think. I've known a long time you can't "do" a project. You do steps. Therefore, much of my focus is on what's the *very next thing* that has to happen to move a project along. And, since I'm a leader, that's typically making a suggestion to somebody."

"So your strategy is to keep very little on your mind."

"Broadly. And that's what you refer to as my appearing 'carefree'." With that he reached into a compartment in the leather arm rest of his seat. He pulled out a new red notepad. "Here," he said sliding it across the table. "Try it. You'll see."

I did try it. And he's right. By moving the things that can't be used or concluded right now into a trusted loop-back system I'm finding I have a lot less 'on my mind' which, in turn, makes my thinking a bit crisper and cleaner. And yes, knowing valuable thoughts aren't going to "escape" leads to a kind of mental relaxation you need to experience to understand. I doubt I'm the sort of person that will ever be truly "carefree" but it's proving an enjoyable and very useful experiment.

If you feel stressed and over committed you should definitely try this technique. I've substituted my smartphone for the little paper pad but it works the same.

Give either a try. You too may never look back.

Think about it...

CHAPTER 20

PREVENTING SYSTEMIC FAILURE (THINGS TO LOOK OUT FOR)

***Originally Published**
October 2008*

Over the last several years one of the nice things about doing the Corpwar newsletter are the conversations I've had with smart, influential people (most of them here in the States but also in the EU and a growing number in the Pac Rim and China). Occasionally they will send along books or papers or links to interviews they've done (Note: apparently being on The Daily Show isn't as much fun as you might think...).

One paper came as a result of a conversation with Bob Prieto. He was the chairman of Parsons Brinkerhoff (think Bechtel). Bob, a nuclear engineer by training, is one of those people you meet and realize, very quickly, you are probably not the smartest person in the room. At the time he was an SVP of Fluor Corporation and was part of the Fluor pitch group for doing work on widening the Panama Canal. That's the scale of Bob's world. Pretty big. Actually pretty huge.

I had called Bob for some advice and the conversation turned to the condition of our economy at the time (it was 2008) and how we got into that dire condition. His take was fascinating. After the call he sent me a paper that uses the construction industry as an analogue to the economy (and vice versa). It's intriguing, especially since it was written around the time the economy tanked. It makes you realize nothing really happens in a vacuum and not much is truly invisible before it becomes a huge, grotesque mess. If you Google Bob Prieto and Black Swans you'll get a good taste of his insights which are remarkably impressive. His papers can also be found at www.PMWorldLibrary.net.

If you take the time to read the short paper it will likely make you think in terms of cause and effect in your own industry and business. When one thing happens, all potential outcomes are somehow effected and possibly remapped entirely. I find particularly useful the paper's framework of the "analogue" (understanding one thing to understand another).

Bob's paper, which at only six pages is very tightly written, addresses several categories of vulnerabilities inherent in highly engineered systems. But the thinking is remarkably portable to systems I guarantee you have, in some form, in your business as well (or your house for that matter).

For example, Bob discusses the vulnerability of tightly coupled systems that go unidentified as such by management. This is very scary because what may look like RANDOM EVENTS can actually be highly coupled. He provides a simple example of a fire in a small building outside of Chicago that disrupted telephone service for much of the country. Why? Because (to quote the paper) "It seems that most transcontinental land-lines passed through that single building and they were destroyed in the fire." Excuse me? How could somebody not know, or know and not do something about, that vulnerability? He gives another example of why the price of anti-freeze went up 300% a while back. Turns out ethylene glycol was made in only two places here in the States and one of them, a small plant in Idaho, burned down with the obvious price result.

Bob also discusses the risk of failing to KISS (Keep It Simple Stupid), inadequate core capacity (and lack of key redundancy), the danger of positive feedback loops (aka progressive failures—which, as an effective recruiter, I was often paid to induce at target companies) and other strikingly relevant concepts. So read the paper. It's short and punchy and can help you ask questions that could potentially save your company, your equity holders, and you.

Bob has graciously given me permission to "spread the paper around" so feel free to forward it. I guarantee it will lead to some interesting and useful conversations.

Read it. Then, think about it...

CHAPTER 21

UPTURNING, IN A DOWNTURN

*Originally Published
In late 2008*

Once again, that Snake Guy advises.

While helping a client quantify the financial rewards of social media I received a call from the reader many of my readers referred to as "that snake guy". This stemmed from his response to a question I asked him back in the toughish times of 2003. I had asked him how someone should behave during an economic downturn. His answer was simple: They should "act like a…snake." This caused a lot of comments from my readers, many using very colorful and pointed language.

Since he was now on the phone, and the country was involved in yet another downturn, this one nasty, I couldn't help but ask him how he would approach things if he were not retired. Below is the brief but useful conversation. Clearly, his tendency toward boisterous, strong opinions has not faded with his fame.

"Well, come on Tal, read your own stuff! An enemy in chaos is prone to remarkable stupidity. Look around. A lot of management can't think on their feet anymore under the best of circumstances and many of the guys that still can are freaked out right now. They're managerially paralyzed, worried about how the board and equity holders will react to good old fashioned decisive CEO behavior. So they're just focused on keeping the ship steady. No unnecessary rocking, thank you very much."

"So, what would you do?"

"Me? Simple. I'd double down. Just double down on where I wanted the company to be."

"You mean as in gambling?"

"That's right. 21."

"But what about pulling in and retrenching?"

"That's for idiots," he said laughing. I could easily picture his self-assured smile. "Look around. Now is a great time to be daring or even audacious. You're always talking about the competition being The Enemy, well, now is the time to figure out what your competition's got that you want and go for it! Just DO IT! Don't act for today. Act for tomorrow. Don't worry about pissing people off because they're gonna be pissed off no matter what you do. Hey, change is gonna happen anyway. You might as well make it in the direction where you want it to go, right?"

"So you would be on the offensive?"

"Damn straight. I'm buying."

"Buying? Now?" This struck me as contrarian but shouldn't have, given the source.

"Sure, nobody is going to be making much money for a while anyway. So making a little less because you bought some assets, well, so f'n what? Just make sure they're the sort of things that help you down the road." He paused then added, "Plus, it shows you're confident."

"Well, brave anyway."

"Of course. But that's a given. You have to be brave. But then good senior managers, hell ALL good managers, have to be. Show me a senior manager that isn't brave and I'll show you a problem."

"A problem to who?"

"Himself. Because if he worked for me he would be looking for a new job."

With that, the conversation moved onto (in approximate order): my daughter in Boulder ("You're kidding! She's now in college? Didn't we advise her on how to grow a babysitting business?"), Gene and Georgetti's steakhouse in Chicago ("I wouldn't say THE best, Tal. But damn close."), Emirates airlines First Class to Dubai ("Actually I've heard there's not much privacy in those new suites but with the right companion it would be fun [to try some funny business], Dubai's Sheikh Rashid Al Maktoum ("What's with all those islands?") and, of course, president elect Obama ("Well, I'm hoping...").

So, it was an interesting conversation. Take a moment and consider—maybe this is the time to "double down" not hunker down. But you will have to be brave.

Think about it...

CHAPTER 22

PRESSURING GENERALS (CEOS) TO DISCLOSE THEIR PLANS. WRONG!

***Originally Published
February 2003***

For 2,500 years smart armies have known: "A great general is unfathomable, his actions having formlessness." Translation: a great general keeps his enemy guessing. A great CEO moves in the same way because the competition wants to prevent him or her from reaching their goal. And reaching intelligent goals is where increases in equity holder value are found (the point of the exercise). But most market share needs to be "taken" just like ground in the battlefield. And taking ground is expensive in countless ways—and even more so if the enemy (your competition) is waiting for you which, if they're good, may be the case.

So the great general (CEO) thinks ahead. Keeps his battle plans vague. Keeps the enemy (the competition) guessing. This allows the great general (CEO) to show up where he isn't expected and that's beautiful competitive technique. That's great corpcraft. And isn't that what we want when we hold equity in a company? Sure.

So why are some criticizing corporate leaders for not publicly disclosing their plans?

Last week the Financial Times (which we hugely admire), published a story with ratings of the annual reports and websites of 50 major companies in the U.S. and Europe. They listed the five "Best" and the five "Worst" companies via a multivariate model (the study was done by Shelly Taylor Associates). The companies were rated on a variety of parameters that heavily weighed how much information they disclosed to readers/viewers. What we found questionable was a major downgrade was bestowed if a chairman didn't discuss, in relative detail, his or her upcoming plans. The more detail the better.

As sharp-end, equity holder oriented competitors, we think that's a bit shortsighted.

Berkshire Hathaway was given the lowest possible rating, the bottom of the list (50th out of 50!) because Warren Buffett didn't exactly rhapsodize about his future plans. Hey, we trust Warren to do right by equity holder value. I don't want to know the details—because we don't want the competition to know any more than they already do. We want Buffett to act like the great CEO (general) he is—be vague, be formless, keep the competition (enemy) off guard, in the smoke and wasting resources, all while our CEO skillfully swings around in the induced fog of competition and *increases the value of the company.*

Think about it...

CHAPTER 23

BILL SWANSON'S "25 UNWRITTEN RULES OF MANAGEMENT"

Originally Published
May 2006

The CEO's Secret Handbook

It seems there have been some allegations that Bill Swanson, the long sitting CEO of Raytheon (a Financial Times Global 500 firm) may have appropriated some of the content for his famous booklet from insufficiently credited sources. In fact, Bill has, at times, openly said he used engineering Professor W. J. King's book written six decades ago for some of the booklet's rules.

However Swanson assembled his list, it doesn't change the fact the 25 rules have proven invaluable to many senior business leaders over the years.

Recently I was working on a senior diversity search where the interviewing of candidates had been subcontracted out to us. Our assignment was to do the interviews and make recommendations (e.g., responding to: "Here, take this stack of resumes and find us the real corporate warriors!"). I like these assignments since I've never met a candidate I couldn't learn something useful from. This project was no exception. In the course of the interviews a couple of the candidates mentioned Mr. Swanson as someone they admired (among other things Swanson is dedicated to diversity in the workplace). Since we did occasional work for the government I'd heard Swanson's name before but never really focused on it other than knowing that, as a manager, he's the real thing. Now curious, I finally looked into it and quickly realized he's the same Swanson that wrote "Swanson's Unwritten Rules of Management" which I had heard rumors about under the name 'The CEO's Secret Handbook'. You may take issue with some of the "rules" and probably have some of your own, but, by and large, it's a powerful list for improving an organization. The list follows.

25 Unwritten Rules of Management

1. Learn to say, "I don't know." If used when appropriate, you will use it often.

2. It is easier to get into something than it is to get out of it.
3. If you are not criticized, you may not be doing much.
4. Look for what is missing. Many know how to improve what's there, but few can see what isn't there.
5. Viewgraph rule: When something appears on a viewgraph (an overhead transparency), assume the world knows about it, and deal with it accordingly.
6. Work for a boss with whom you are comfortable telling it like it is (AKA Truth to Power - TN). Remember that you can't pick your relatives, but you can pick your boss.
7. Constantly review developments to make sure that the actual benefits are what they are supposed to be. Avoid Newton's Law.
8. However menial and trivial your early assignments may appear, give them your best efforts.
9. Persistence or tenacity is the disposition to persevere in spite of difficulties, discouragement, or indifference. Don't be known as a good starter but a poor finisher.
10. In completing a project, don't wait for others; go after them, and make sure it gets done.
11. Confirm your instructions and the commitments of others in writing. Don't assume it will get done!

12. Don't be timid; speak up. Express yourself, and promote your ideas.
13. Practice shows that those who speak the most knowingly and confidently often end up with the assignment to get it done.
14. Strive for brevity and clarity in oral and written reports.
15. Be extremely careful of the accuracy of your statements.
16. Don't overlook the fact that you are working for a boss. Keep him or her informed. Avoid surprises! Whatever the boss wants takes top priority.
17. Promises, schedules, and estimates are important instruments in a well-ordered business. You must make promises. Don't lean on the often-used phrase, "I can't estimate it because it depends upon many uncertain factors."
18. Never direct a complaint to the top. A serious offense is to "cc" a person's boss.
19. When dealing with outsiders, remember that you represent the company. Be careful of your commitments. (Under promise, over deliver. - TN)
20. Cultivate the habit of "boiling matters down" to the simplest terms. An elevator speech is the best way.
21. Don't get excited in engineering emergencies. Keep your feet on the ground.

22. Cultivate the habit of making quick, clean-cut decisions.
23. When making decisions, the pros are much easier to deal with than the cons. Your boss wants to see the cons also.
24. Don't ever lose your sense of humor.
25. Have fun at what you do. It will reflect in your work. No one likes a grump except another grump.

Think about it...

"Cashing a paycheck is an oath to perform your best."

-T. Newhart

CHAPTER 24

NORMAL VS. EXTRAORDINARY PERFORMANCE (VS. VANITY)

Originally Published
March 2003

There was a lot of mail from people that didn't understand the CEO's snake comment a while back about his not being afraid of personal embarrassment and how that opened up a lot of opportunities for him and his company, which is very large and successful.

The underlying issue is normal vs. extraordinary performance and it's the same in a military or commercial battle. Slow, steady gains come from solid, methodical performance. And that's great. However, *big gains* often require audacity and if they go wrong, well, it can be humiliating to the CEO. So CEOs often take a pass on such moves, taking the safer route instead. That said, a great CEO never forgets he or she is a servant of the stakeholders. Sometimes he or she MUST take chances and vanity should be the last thing on their mind.

> *"The general (CEO) who advances without coveting fame and retreats without fearing disgrace, whose only thought is to protect his country (the company and employees) and do good service for his sovereign (chairman), is the jewel of the kingdom (equity holders)."*
>
> *Sun Tzu*

An old battlefield saying forgotten by many (R.I.P.) dot.com CEOs in the early days of the Internet: *"The easy way is always mined."*

Think about it…

CHAPTER 25

HOLIDAY COMMENTS ABOUT CORPORATE RESPONSIBILITY

Originally Published
December 2003

A Broader Perspective on Corporate Governance
"The Global Sullivan Principles"

Any reader of this occasional newsletter knows the focus is on providing executives with techniques to provide stakeholders with sustainable increases in the value of their equity. We often do this by converting key battle tactics to business strategy and by showing the behaviors of history's great generals. We get feedback that this has proven useful as it has helped readers ask themselves questions that have resulted in action items ultimately enriching their stakeholders. That's gratifying.

It's hard to find any group more focused on helping clients enrich their equity holders than we are, and by extension, our core readers. They are an impressive group.

Of course we also get asked questions ourselves. One of the most frequent is, "But what about the Big Picture? What about corporate governance?"

What does the board DO other than work together, in a principled manner, to help the company create and maintain customers for the benefit of the stakeholders? The point is, with the power large companies have today perhaps enriching the stakeholder isn't enough—maybe that's just the beginning.

Ok, this holiday season, with Saddam Hussein now in jail, and with 2004 looking better, we'd like to suggest something...

Back in 1971 a Baptist minister by the name of Leon Sullivan joined the board of General Motors (Sullivan was the first African-American on the board of a major US corporation). At the time General Motors was the largest employer of blacks in South Africa. Sullivan used his position on the board to oppose apartheid, the set of official policies in the Republic of South Africa that discriminated against nonwhites. To do this he created the Sullivan Principles in 1977 which were a set of ethical guidelines for companies operating in South Africa. Where other reformers, such as Nelson Mandela, had failed, the Sullivan Principles were instrumental in bringing about the ultimate dismantling of apartheid. The country has flourished since. (I've worked there and greatly enjoyed both the country and its varied people.)

How did he do it? Simple. Economic pressure. Sullivan knew multinationals and large, nongovernmental entities, are growing in power where nation states are increasingly having a difficult time achieving co-operative solutions. Sullivan mobilized over a 100 companies to leave South Africa and apartheid eventually crumbled. That's a simplification but the Sullivan Principles are credited as the flashpoint.

In 1999, not long before his death, Rev. Sullivan and United Nations Secretary General Kofi Annan, introduced a revised set of ethical operating guidelines called the Global Sullivan Principles of Corporate Responsibility. These expanded guidelines call for multinationals to take a more active role in the advancement of social justice.

But if you read them, and think about them, you can see the Principles provide a sensible framework and filter set for balanced corporate behavior on a global basis. It's easy to see why many large and admirable companies have adopted the guidelines and why some significant institutional investors have chosen to focus on investing in companies that follow the principles. Have a look and give it a thought.

Happy Holidays and Happy New Year—-and cheers to a strong 2004. –Tal Newhart

The Global Sullivan Principals
Announced November 2, 1999 at the United Nations, New York City

As a company which endorses the Global Sullivan Principles we will respect the law, and as a responsible member of society we will apply these Principles with integrity consistent with the legitimate role of business. We will develop and implement company policies, procedures, training and internal reporting structures to ensure commitment to these principles throughout our organization. We believe the application of these Principles will achieve greater tolerance and better understanding among peoples, and advance the culture of peace.

Accordingly, we will:

- Express our support for universal human rights and, particularly, those of our employees, the communities within which we operate, and parties with whom we do business.
- Promote equal opportunity for our employees at all levels of the company with respect to issues such as color, race, gender, age, ethnicity or religious beliefs, and operate without unacceptable worker treatment such as the exploitation of children, physical punishment, female abuse, involuntary servitude, or other forms of abuse.
- Respect our employees' voluntary freedom of association.

- Compensate our employees to enable them to meet at least their basic needs and provide the opportunity to improve their skill and capability in order to raise their social and economic opportunities.
- Provide a safe and healthy workplace; protect human health and the environment; and promote sustainable development.
- Promote fair competition including respect for intellectual and other property rights, and not offer, pay or accept bribes.
- Work with governments and communities in which we do business to improve the quality of life in those communities - their educational, cultural, economic and social wellbeing and seek to provide training and opportunities for workers from disadvantaged backgrounds.
- Promote the application of these principles by those with whom we do business.
- We will be transparent in our implementation of these principles and provide information which demonstrates publicly our commitment to them.

Think about it...

CHAPTER 26

"CAPITALIST GONE WILD!!"

**Originally Published
December 2003**

*Trapped in a Toys-R-Us parking lot
Or
How I almost got beat up in a holiday parking lot for
spreading FGS (Financial Good Sense)*

Last Wednesday (12/17/2003) I was walking up to my car in the local Toys-R-Us parking lot (those that say the economy isn't improving should try to park at a toy store this holiday season) and was sagging under my efforts to add to Toys-R-Us' equity holder value.

As I approached my car I noticed somebody was peering in its windows. Behind my car was a black

Mercedes S600 stopped, engine running, with the driver door open. Clearly it was the owner looking into my car's windows. This was curious. While my car is nice it's not unusual for the local demographic. I noted the guy's sharply tailored Prada suit.

"Hi, can I help you?" I said walking up with a big holiday smile (genuine at this point).

"Is this yours?" he said nodding sharply toward the car.

"Yes," I answered, still holding my colorful and burgeoning shopping bags.

He pointed at the license plate, "You put out this newsletter?"

I looked at the license plate which clearly references this blog. Also the license plate frame spells out my company's name. Obviously my cover was blown! "Sure. Are you a reader?"

"Well I think your last issue about corporate responsibility was full of sh*t!" (Referring to The Sullivan Principles)

His comment surprised me because there were kids and parents around. Then somebody tooted their horn as his stopped car was fouling up traffic in the busy parking lot.

"Well, why don't you park and we'll talk about it." I said this knowing the next parking spot was probably in the next city, LOL.

"No, this'll just take a second," he snapped glancing at the cars wisely backing up. "You guys say you're all for maximizing equity holder value but by advocating that companies I invest in spend money on social BS, well, that's basically like stealing from me. Really, that's just liberal bullsh*t." He started moving back towards his car door to get in. "That's all I wanted to say."

As he was about to get in his car I said, "Can I ask you something?"

"Yeah. *What?*"

I smiled. "Would you like my parking place?"

He scowled, called me a nasty name (a body part), then climbed into the $120,000 car and roared off. Still standing there with my packages I shook my head as if to wake up. While it felt like an hour or so the whole scene had taken only a few seconds. Traffic started moving again. The world seemed safer.

Now, it would be simple to just say that the fellow was having a bad day (rare holiday parking spots being the supreme annoyance they are) and I was an easy target. But the fact is at last count we've gotten over 100 e-mails saying basically the same thing: 'business is tough-it's irresponsible to suggest spending any corporate resources on non-essentials like a company's social responsibility programs."

Ok, let's think about Corporate Social Responsibility (CSR) this way…

Had the gentlemen in the parking lot stuck around I would have asked him some simple questions such as:

1. Do you think it would be ok with equity holders for a company to reject the notion that people

of different races, gender, or sexual orientation can add value to a company and therefore block them from working there?
2. Do you think it would be ok with equity holders for a company to pay fines and huge legal fees for polluting?
3. Do you think it's ok to attract the negative attention of the press and risk revenue sucking boycotts?
4. Do you think it would be ok with equity holders that a company turn its back on the growing number of customers that prefer doing business with companies that try to improve society and take care of the environment rather than simply exploiting them for profit?
5. Etc. Etc. Etc.

Frankly, it sounds to us like spending money on social responsibility programs can be a good investment rather than just the reckless squandering of corporate resources some seem to believe!

Think about it...

Happy Holidays,
   Tal

CHAPTER 27

A USEFUL BUSINESS WEAPON CALLED FUD

Originally Published
November 2004

Alexis de Tocqueville observed that it is easier for the world to accept a simple lie than a complex truth. Hannibal knew the same thing 1,000 years earlier. Today, if your company is in a serious jam, this human weakness can be very useful.

Even at the best companies things occasionally go wrong. You've messed up. Taken your eyes off the ball. And of course the competition is right there to exploit your faltering. That's the other CEO/general's job. Exploit your weakness. If he or she's really good or has good spies (the legal kind—we'll cover them briefly below and in detail some other time) they may know you're in trouble even before you do! That's a tough opponent for sure. The clock's ticking even louder than normal.

So you're losing customers, maybe not many yet, but there's talk of a better way than yours out there. You don't have much time and you are behind the development curve. Things are grim. What do you do?

After kicking Development's rear you can do what IBM did when computer architect Gene Amdahl jumped ship in September of 1970 to start Amdahl. You generate "FUD". In fact FUD victim Gene came up with the term. It stands for the "Fear, Uncertainty and Doubt". IBM salespeople would skillfully plant FUD in the minds of prospective Amdahl customers. IBM knew Amdahl was brilliant and his starting another mainframe company could easily cause IBM serious problems. So they put the word out, via back and side-channels, that Amdahl's computers were somehow risky. It worked. Once again IBM made IBM the "safe" choice. "Why take a chance? Why change? Stick with us. We'll take care of you." The fact was Gene's computers were cheaper and faster but IBM successfully created a dark, foreboding cloud over them. This slowed Amdahl down and provided protection to IBM.

Microsoft has made an art form out of FUD (the term is frequently used in the tech arena) in their battles to fight the very real threats of Linux and Open Source. In fact Microsoft even discusses its value in leaked internal memos as a tool in the Linux and Open Source wars.

Finally, in the beginning, many people believed, and some still do, that Larry Ellison's move to buy PeopleSoft was just elaborate FUD. The idea was that if PeopleSoft became a part of Oracle, PeopleSoft software would wither. The object, of course, was to inhibit the purchase of PeopleSoft products (another moral is to 'never mess with Larry', but that's another story). And it worked.

The point is it doesn't take much 'Fear, Uncertainty and Doubt' to freeze the use of a corporate checkbook, especially for a "risky" resource. And that's the object here.

FUD is particularly useful for the large company battling a smaller one, because to established customers the "new small guy" generally feels a bit risky anyway. The majority of the readers of this newsletter are in positions of importance in large companies, many of them multinationals (the balance largely entrepreneurs). As we all know big companies are seldom as nimble as small ones. This can give the small company a tactical advantage. They can occasionally get a technically superior product or service out quicker than you can. Plus, as we've detailed previously, a smart small company can show up where you don't expect them—where you are somehow weak—and have no, or insufficient, in-place defenses against them. This allows the small guy to gain a foothold in your territory (what Sun Tzu called "Ground"). It's David taking a swipe at Goliath. Again.

So, what do you do? Your product (software, drug, widget) is late. The "why" is secondary even though you can dial that into more FUD ("Our new drug is still 6 months out but it'll be a revolution. Why start your patients on something new only to have to change them later for something better?"). What you really need to do, RIGHT NOW, is slow down the competition before they get share because it's too expensive getting it back, and sometimes you can't. Especially if what they are selling really is better—hey, it happens. Never forget, a little bit better is often enough to induce customer flight.

Now is a time that FUD can be very useful. And yes, we could discuss the ethicalness of FUD till the next equity holder's meeting but if we ask them don't we know what the answer is likely to be? And they are the owners. They want the maximum return possible and it's our job to provide them with it to the maximum degree that is legal. Just don't go over the edge. Happily you don't really have to.

You don't even need to lie here to win, folks. All you have to do is create any or all of Fear, Uncertainty and Doubt. And there are lots of ways to do that. One of the simplest is by asking the right question. If you discern they are a credible new threat, find out what the David company fears most. To find out, cruise social media. It's u-n-b-e-l-i-e-v-a-b-l-e what you can turn up following a competitor's loquacious employees chatting, sometimes anonymously, about what their company is up to. We frequently monitor social platforms for clients and it's scary what employees freely divulge. Read a couple of levels below the line in their press releases. Talk with their suppliers, new customers, old employees. And finally just put yourself in their shoes—what would you be afraid of? You're in the same business. You probably know what he or she sweats the target customers might find out. That's what you toss into the spin machine, plant the seeds to slightly disorient and leave the rest to the imagination of the David's potential new customers (your existing and targeted ones). *Never forget that refuting takes a lot more resources than asserting.* Ask any Presidential campaigner.

Think about it...

CHAPTER 28

FUD UPDATE

Originally Published
October 2005

Victim: the Apple iPod Nano
(A vivid example of how FUD works)

Last November I did a Corpwar issue on FUD (Fear, Uncertainty & Doubt) as a competitive weapon. Basically I described how it works and why it's such an effective tool for giving your competitors a very bad day. It's cheap and simple. For better or worse there's no question FUD is one of the attack dogs of the modern corporate battlefield. A true corporate warfare terror weapon. And corporate warriors need to know how to use it.

An interesting thing happened after we sent that FUD issue out. We immediately received several calls asking if we would help engineer FUD "campaigns" (an LOL euphemism for "attacks") against the callers' competitors. Since the calls came from longtime readers I took the requests seriously but declined. I declined not because I have anything against the tool but because I knew, in at least two cases, the idea was to use heavy FUD against other Corpwar readers, one of which is also a search client of mine and I'm extremely protective of my clients. So, after a couple of technical conversations, we took a firm pass. Unfortunately, I think one of those conversations was later put to effective use...

Let's flash forward to early last week.

I got a call from a reader that's a senior executive in the computer and music industry. He remembered the FUD piece and asked me if I would take a look at what's happening to Apple's brand new iPod Nano. The iPod Nano is a nifty little music player that basically blows away everything else in its category. In general, iPods have a market share of between 40%-70% depending upon who you ask. The Nano is designed to extend that dominance down into the lower end of the market where a variety of smaller, non-disk drive players are scrapping violently for sales. Naturally a new, and essentially perfect product (the Nano), put out by the industry Death Star, is very, very bad news to the scrappers desperately chiseling away for share in the category.

So, what does a real Corporate Warrior do? Simple: you FUD the new product. If all else fails, think like a guerilla fighter. Guerilla warfare, by its amorphous and cost-effective nature, is extremely hard for the incumbent to effectively battle against.

A rumor suddenly started circulating a couple of weeks ago that the iPod Nano has a particularly scratchable screen and that they could even shatter. The rumor quickly spread that the scratching issue was so bad that if you left the Nano in your pocket (where music players frequently live) the screen could quickly become marred to the point you could barely read the underlying text rendering it almost unusable. Supposedly this would happen even if the pocket was empty other than the Nano. (I could never figure this out.) I asked the fellow how the polymer in the Nano's screen differed from other iPods (none of which have a scratching issue) and he laughed, vaguely amazed: "It's the same stuff!" He added there was a minor supplier issue with some breaking screens but that was being fixed immediately and they were repairing the Nanos that had broken. It was the rumor of the screens being so easily scratched that was the expensive issue. Some potential buyers were reacting as expected—holding off. (The typical potential customer reaction to well-crafted FUD is to execute an immediate full stop).

His question was simple: Did I know anything about who might be spreading the rumors (e.g. the

FUD)? Well, in fact, maybe. But what's the difference? The attacker didn't even have to explicitly lie. It IS possible to scratch the Nano's screen (of course you can scratch a diamond too). The damage is done. FUD can be modeled via a contagion model because it spreads like a biological agent moving through a living population. The more closed-in the population the faster the contagion moves. And few things move like good FUD since it doesn't require "old fashioned" physical distribution (air, touch, etc.) especially when it breaks out into the press and social media spaces where it can become an epidemic of disinformation in a couple of hours. These days FUD can travel at almost the speed of light because that's how fast data can move along optical fiber. Think about it. It's scary. But it's also an opportunity for the true corporate warrior that needs to make, or protect sales, to survive. Few things can slow a competitor down, or even stop them altogether, like well-crafted FUD. Period. It's Very Nasty Stuff. It's electronic anthrax.

So here it is just a few weeks in and the iPod Nano is felt by many to be somehow "delicate" (this is what it all factors down to). And that's pretty terrible for a portable music player. Although Apple's recent stock performance was blamed on the downgrading by Merrill some blamed it on the perception that the new product has problems and this might somehow prove Apple was pushing new products to market too quickly, e.g. the perceived problems with the Nano's screen somehow demonstrating Apple was becoming reckless.

The funny thing (well, sort of funny) is the caller naturally thought that it might be one of Apple's big competitors that had initiated the FUD. Not necessarily. Knowing how flexible FUD can be in the hands of a clever corporate warrior, my response was simple: "Or, look for somebody very small. Somebody new that needs revenues badly and that can make them by mitigating a supposed flaw in the Nano's construction. Look around. They will be advertising, or somehow in the press or on social media, for solving the problem." "You mean like a [music player] case maker or screen protector manufacturer?" "Exactly," I answered. I further described that a lot of people will buy the high utility Nano even if they think it has problems and, predictably, they will attempt to mitigate the problem via an accessory (a very American response, especially for the younger demographic). It's the people on the fence that will be swayed by the FUD not to buy (many people are eager to find reasons not to spend money and they are happy to wait for the social proof provided by early adopters and, even then, may have actionable doubts). And there are more than a few of them. (Note: I'm not one of them. I bought a Nano for my plane, then one for each family member. It's immensely excellent and none of my hyperactive clan have yet to see any screen marring whatsoever.) But causing potential buyers to delay may just be a collateral effect. The real FUD benefactor here is the accessory maker who now has an accessory that's perceived of as a necessity. Very clever. Very good FUD unless you're an Apple equity holder waiting for reality to overcome the FUD. (This often happens but it can be a very expensive wait, which is also, of course, an access window for still others that can even position against the "flaw".)

The underlying lesson here is it didn't take much effort on the front end to create the Fear, Uncertainly and Doubt. And it was created fast (in fact, REALLY FAST) and cheaply.

Think about this the next time you're taking on somebody much bigger, or you're really big yourself and feeling complacent and untouchable.

Seriously, think about it…

CHAPTER 29

MORE LESSONS FROM THE CORPORATE BATTLEFIELD WITH CLIENT X

Originally Published in 2010

AKA: Recovering the Spear Tip

[Note: This adventure/lesson happened in January 2009 before I came out to California from Chicago for the winter. It has taken this long to get it cleared with the client. When I passed it by him he made some minor changes and cuts. The reasons are obvious.]

One day early last week my phone rang. It was still dark outside. I looked at the time on the phone. It was 5:00 AM. I recognized the hiss of an in-flight phone. "Hello?"

"What are you doing for the next few hours?" The voice was assured and backed with a smile. I recognized it instantly as many in his industry might.

"I'm meeting you in The Loop to discuss those candidates and the book. Why?"

"Slight change of plans. Meet me at the airport in Wheeling at about 6:30. We'll be back by noon or so. We can work on the plane."

I sat up in bed and rubbed my eyes. Part of me said I was too old for this and another part was certainly intrigued. "Ok. I'm in. Where are we going?"

"Southeast."

"Ah, why?"

"Because yesterday afternoon somebody became the most important person in my company and it wasn't me!"

This was interesting because I was on the phone with the high profile CEO of a Fortune company. "And who would that be?"

"A guy on one of our loading docks."

"A guy on one of your loading docks became the most important person in your company?" I asked.

"Yeah. Great, isn't it! Just like that. He became The Spear. I need to go down and thank him in person. I'll have the co-pilot pick us up some mac griddles across from the airport. There's nothing on here except Starbuck's and some sugar packets. See you at the south end." And with that the phone went dead. As I got dressed and headed to my car I wondered what a "mac griddle" was.

Ninety minutes later I was climbing into a small, idling jet north of Chicago. One of the pilots pulled the steps up behind me and sealed the door. My host, we'll call him Jack (not his real name), was sitting there in sneakers, jeans and a golf jacket. He was watching a PowerPoint show on a bulkhead mounted LCD screen. He handed me a greasy hamburger-like thing and pointed to an adjacent seat. A few minutes later we were in a very steep climb heading out over Lake Michigan.

After some small talk and the luridly fattening repast I nodded toward the screen while sipping the fresh coffee the co-pilot had handed me. Jack was on his third PowerPoint show. Using a hand remote he flicked through the slides with strobe-like speed. Yet every few slides he would back-up, reread the slide, then march forward. It was clear he was absorbing the content.

He looked over at me while pointing the controller toward the screen. "This is such BS. It's crazy how many guys think they can effectively manage this way."

"What way is that?" I asked.

"By hiding."

"Hiding? In what sense?"

"You know. Trying to manage people while hiding behind a desk. Behind report-tos. Behind these damn things," he said waving again at the PowerPoint show. "The best lesson I've ever learned about leadership is that true leadership requires LEADING for God's sake. And a lot of that is face to face where somebody's expression can say something that may never come out of their mouth."

"Like what?" I asked.

"Like you're full of sh*t!"

"But those are the ones you really want," I said. "The ones that say it, but perhaps with less eloquence. Truth to power, and all."

"But they're rare. Too rare," he said.

"You told me at the Christmas party that 'a manager occasionally has to be seen to be heard,' remember that?" I asked.

"Sure. And that the good ones, like your Good generals, manage from the front. Not always. But often. And that's kind of what we're doing today. I'm going out to the front to earn my paycheck and take care of my equity holders."

He switched the monitor over to CNN and said, "Ok, who do you have for me?" and we started going over what we were scheduled to cover later that morning downtown.

Two hours later the big white Suburban that had picked us up at the narrow strip pulled around the back of a low, non-descript complex that looked like a thousand others I'd seen. I noticed there were cross coverage CCT cameras everywhere. The rear gate's security guard required a picture ID despite the fact we were in a company car driven by a company driver carrying the distinctive CEO. Under a crisp blue sky we were driven over beside the multi-bay loading dock. There were two men obviously waiting for us up on the platform.

Before we climbed out my host looked at me and smiled. "You know you wrote about this very thing in that e-rag you do." He pointed through the SUV's side window to the two men "You see the guy on the right?" I focused on the burly black man. He was wearing the stout clothing of somebody that toiled physically for a living. He stood on the freight dock like he had owned it for many years. It was his office. On his face was a relaxed, confident smile as he chatted with the man beside him who had on a dress shirt and sedate tie. Jack said, "Yesterday afternoon that receiving agent was the most important man in the company. He became the tip of the spear."

"And we're here...why? To say thank you?" I asked thinking that was pretty cool but also calculating the cost of the jet fuel and identified McGriddles.

The boss smiled and laughed. "Of course. And naturally to take the spear back!"

And with that we got out and climbed up onto the dock. Jack was carrying a heavy paper bag I'd noticed on the plane.

After introductions Jack turned to the receiving agent, "So what happened, exactly?"

"Well, sir, it was just like any other delivery except for the numbers on the crate. They didn't match the manifest."

"So, if you thought it wasn't for us why did you sign for it? I can't imagine that's policy."

"Because he," he said motioning toward his supervisor "put up a sign in the break room that said 'Think like an equity holder.' I thought if I was an equity holder I'd want to know what was in a box that was accidentally delivered here rather than to our competition."

Jack smiled and laughed quietly. He faced me as he held out his hands palms up as if presenting the receiving agent: "See Tal, right here, right now, the most important person in the entire company." Jack then reached out and said "Thank you!" He warmly shook the agent's enormous hand again. "Now where is it?"

The four of us walked into a locked room off to the side of the loading bays. The wooden crate, a heavy looking five foot cube on a synthetic pallet, looked like any other. There was no obvious way in. The top was fastened down by a dozen or so screws. The plain room was completely empty other than the box.

Resting his hands on it Jack looked at the two men and asked, "Nobody has touched this?" They both shook their heads. "Who else knows it's here?"

The supervisor, who was a bit unnerved by the fact he was in the company of the CEO, answered the question,

"Just the four of us, [the plant manager] that called your office, and the freight company that delivered it."

"Ok, let's keep it that way," Jack said. "And thanks, I'll take it from here." The dock supervisor asked if Jack would need a screwdriver and Jack replied, with a smile, "No, of course not." The door closed behind us. The room was dim and dusty. I wasn't feeling particularly comfortable.

"Now what?" I asked.

"I'm going to take the spear back. I'll meet you out on the dock," he nodded toward the door.

That was certainly my cue and I walked back out into the fresh air and chatted blandly with the supervisor. The agent signed in a couple of deliveries as we watched. He moved with an easy, fluid expertise. A half hour later I saw Jack walking briskly towards us from around the far side of the building. He must have gone further inside onto the production floor and out the front through the front offices. I realized it was now impossible to tell how long he had been with the crate even if he'd had a way to open it.

Jack was smiling and spoke to the super. "Look, call the courier and tell them they have a misdelivery. Be sure they pick it up today."

After thanking the receiving agent and supervisor again we climbed back into the SUV and headed for the small airport. Jack and I were both quiet. We both accepted the fact there was a big hairy rhinoceros in the corner we were choosing not to discuss. And that was ok with me. My services have always included a very high degree of discretion, so the silence was natural, even expected.

A few minutes later we pulled up to the waiting jet. As we walked towards it Jack turned around and took a few steps back towards a metal trash can by the gate. There was a heavy thud. I smiled. I guess I'll never know for certain what was in the bag but I'm pretty sure I know the sound of a tossed battery powered screw driver when I hear it.

Think about it…

CHAPTER 30

SOME BASIC RULES OF CORPORATE WARFARE

Originally Published
December 2011

(Things to Include in a Corporate Warrior's Toolkit)

Last week I was invited to dinner by two longtime readers of this newsletter that happened to be in town. Both are well known as being effective capitalists on a large scale. Both have, on occasion, been loudly criticized for being a bit on the savage side. Victors often are. That said, they have both done an outstanding long-term job of driving increasing equity holder value so, in my book, they are ok guys. I wrote about a meeting with one of them in the chapter titled: How a Famous CEO Stays So Calm.

After agreeing on The Fundamental Rule ("add value to the customer") we got into a lengthy discussion about competitive behaviors and philosophies for competing to win in today's, and tomorrow's, marketplace. I started scribbling out notes and have put the tenets into the list below. It was an interesting and useful evening to say the least.

I encourage you to forward this to your staff since, eventually, the good of a competitive mindset, shared by all, reaches down and out to the tiniest roots in a world-class company and eventually finds its way out to the equity holders' wallets.

This is a good basic list to pedal through while making any competitive decision. Keep it handy:

1. Act according to a plan only after a thorough analysis of the possible outcomes.
2. Minimize damage to the competition. Capturing him intact will typically maximize your gain (said from an M&A perspective but useful elsewhere).
3. Maximize profit by minimizing the use of force, which is expensive. Force is more efficient when not actually used. The optics of known, but withheld force, are onerous.
4. Weaken your competition before engagement (hire away his most valuable executives, disrupt

his supplies, maybe spread around some FUD, etc.). This effectively strengthens you.
5. Shape, or control, your competition. Make him do things he would not normally do (lure him into undesirable markets, force up his costs, make him trip). While often fun to do, these things should all be designed to increase your advantage and relate to a specific goal of some sort and not just to amuse you (Though that does have value. We work hard and life is short. Have fun. - Tal)
6. Analyze every possible course of action for the advantages and disadvantages of every possible outcome. Endeavor to convert your own disadvantages into advantages, and your enemy's advantages into disadvantages.
7. Use your enemy's own psychological and philosophical structures against him. Somewhat tough to do (and can backfire badly) but when successful this will rattle him and may have him gasping, "But hey, I thought we were the good guys!"
8. When attacking/moving into a new market be extremely sensitive to any changes and adapt accordingly. "Be like water" (adapt to the terrain). Keep in mind you're probably being watched so ask yourself "What do they see and what can they conclude from what they see?" Then ask, "How can I modify what they see to my advantage?"

9. Attack with sufficient strength where you are not expected. Note: One of my hosts suggested using overwhelming force to debilitate the opposition. The other thought this would suggest you had misjudged the situation and thus wasted resources. I agree with the later. Less waste and destruction means more profit for you and yours.
10. Try to achieve your goals via indirect methods your competition doesn't expect. Again, always be "unfathomable". If you are unfathomable your competition will have a very difficult time effectively planning and executing against you.
11. Speed is everything. Always be asking yourself "How can I get this done quicker without more costs." Quicker wars (of all kinds, even with kids I'm still learning) are cheaper.
12. Think it through. Never forget that battles are won or lost before they are fought.

The list is longer but these are the easy-to-deploy heavies. It's a quick list when you get used to the "mode of thinking".

Think about it…

> *I had a useful sign made for my office wall: "Business Bullets are fast. Fire first."*

> *-T. Newhart*

CHAPTER 31

HOW A FORTUNE 500 CEO HELPS CHANGE HAPPEN IN 7 STEPS

Originally Published
August 2012

Before the client pulled the limo's door closed he looked up at me and said, "I'll send the steps to your phone. Give me about 15 minutes." He then looked at the candidate standing beside me and said, "Welcome aboard! Work it out with him," he said nodding toward me. He added a quick "Thanks!" then smiled and waved to a couple of passersby that recognized him. With that he drew the car's door closed as it pulled away from the Four Seasons toward Chicago's Midway Airport.

The candidate and I stood on the windy sidewalk watching the car. It had been a long interview. I hadn't been hired to find the candidates for the job. This time I was sent a short list of high profile managers to entice into possibly working for the fellow in the car. Most of the people on the list receive this newsletter so it was pretty straightforward. I did the video screening interviews then set up and facilitated the final interviews like this one. This was all done quickly, with no fanfare, and with the hermetic confidentiality my clients expect from me.

Leaning against the wind the tall candidate looked at me. "I guess that means I got the job." He paused and added, "Right?" he said with a hint of laughter.

I put out my hand and shook his. I'd been through this oddness before. He hadn't. I nodded. "Oh, yes," I said, adding, "Congratulations! You're in for an interesting 48 months." I looked around him and signaled the doorman. A cab materialized almost out of thin air. As the candidate climbed in we shook hands again and I said, "We'll get the letter over in the morning. You'll like the final terms."

A moment later he was headed toward O'Hare. I turned and went back into the hotel. Taking the elevator up to the Seasons Lounge, I ordered a drink and fell into one of the cushy chairs.

The conversation that afternoon had ranged from Little League to the Army's concept of VUCA (Volatility, Uncertainty, Complexity and Ambiguity) to the difference between action and change. "Action is often meaningless," the client said in his well known, matter-of-fact manner. "Change is what counts." We explored the importance of getting inside your competition's decision cycle, the value of "ground truth" and the importance of empowering all your teams with what he (and the Army) called an electronic, real-time RCP, or Relevant Common Picture "so that everybody makes decisions from the same information" (the candidate had implemented a similar system with such granularity he could predict what his competition was going to do often even before they knew themselves—awesome). Like I said, it had been an intensely engaging afternoon. There was a reason my head throbbed.

The phone in my jacket pocket vibrated. I took it out and downloaded the note. Here is what it said: (Note: Some of the text was in a different font and I could see I wasn't the only person to get a version of this particular missive. The list is reproduced here with his permission and it can be forwarded by any Corpwar reader that wants to do so.)

Tal, I have found there are typically at least 7 stages to making a change in an organization. I always try to do all of them since over the years I've found skipping any of the stages reduces the chances of eventual success. This isn't just for the big glory moves either. It works at all levels. All my senior managers understand, and use, some version of the list.

1. **Time**. The change has to happen soon. Make sure you get across why it's a good thing. If you have communicated the benefits properly you shouldn't need your boot tips.
2. **Team**. I get a team together, preferably where everybody knows and has worked with each other, to see the thing through, soup to nuts; from the beginning all the way through to the eventual consumer, whether internal or external. Pick the team wisely. Make sure there are some dissenters. You don't want everybody thinking alike. You need the idea to be rigorously challenged internally. I use that Gen. Patton quote you sent out. ("If everyone is thinking alike, somebody isn't thinking." -General George Patton, Jr.)
3. **Vision of the future**. Convey your vision to your teams. If you don't have a vision, work with your trusted resources to develop one. If you still don't have one, do your equity holders a favor and help find your replacement.
4. **Communication**. Make sure everybody in the enterprise/group knows what the vision is.
5. **Empower**. Make sure everybody can move their area toward the vision. This way you can converge on it on multiple tracks. There should be a lot of work in parallel. Think digital. Analog is yesterday.

6. **Interim goals**. If the vision is too far off people may not be sufficiently motivated. Dial in sub-goals so they can occasionally taste their own momentum toward the ultimate prize. People prefer to reach for what they can actually touch; it's ok to keep it beyond their grasp, just not too far or too often.
7. **Reinforce**. When the change has been achieved keep it high profile until it is assimilated into the organization or group. Get it organic as soon as possible. It has to be part of the walls. Part of the mindset. The culture.

Get the paperwork to that guy ASAP. I like him. As you said last night, "He gets it."

With that I dropped the phone into my pocket, paid the bill and left for home. Interesting day.

—END—

ADDENDUM: SOME INTERESTING AND USEFUL INTERVIEWS

THE ETHICAL HACKER INTERVIEW

Originally Published
Summer 2014

ASSIGNMENT: Find an accomplished ethical hacker for a contract
LOCATION: Woodside, CA
CLIENT: A large technology company

Note: Parts of this post have been redacted/changed to obscure certain identifying details. John isn't the candidate's real name. The car wasn't white. Technology explanations and clarifications are in square brackets.

SUMMARY: I was tasked with finding a skilled 'white hat' hacker (e.g. an ethical hacker with or without a

CEH certificate) for a specific task, which I can't disclose. The client was one of the most affluent, influential senior executives on the U.S. West Coast. The track down and reference checking took a month and compensated skills proofing (e.g. "find the data files that pertain to X project at this physical address [a distant, client owned complex]") took another couple of weeks. Three candidates were short-listed; this is the one that eventually got the gig, which was difficult and lucrative. This was the second day of the face-to-face interview and getting to know him had been fun. The first morning, after showing me how he detected a foreign company had installed a backdoor on his client's server, he secretly turned on the notebook microphone in the rival COO's office so we could hear a meeting going on ("This is trivial and don't judge. It's his own medicine!"). After the demonstration he described how the weirdest thing he ever hacked was an in situ anesthesia device. Acknowledging my alarmed expression over this he shrugged and grinning, said, "Hey, come on, it had an Internet connection! I couldn't just ignore it!" A genuinely scary point. Funny guy though.

The white Lamborghini coasted to a stop. The young driver, John, looked over at me and said, "Well, that didn't sound good!"

It was a vast understatement. A few moments before we had been screeching along Skyline Boulevard above Palo Alto, California. The day was beautiful. No traffic. The sound of the ridiculously expensive car was intoxicating.

Then the fun stopped with a loud POP, a weird screech followed by eerie silence. We were going fast enough that we were able to coast off Skyline and down a side road surrounded by massive redwoods. It was mostly dark and moist with pools of light on the narrow lane.

A minute later we were standing behind the low car looking down into the opened rear engine compartment. The engine was making a cracking sound as it cooled off. It was smoking and smelled bad. We weren't going anywhere.

John looked up at me with his boyish face, "What do you think?"

All I could do was nod and say, conclusively, "Expensive."

He pulled out a phone. In two days I hadn't seen this one. It was an old flippy, almost an antique (and therefore devoid of a GPS chip). In a resigned voice he said, "Yeah. I figured. I'll call him." He walked a short distance away into a shaft of light between the tall trees and called the car's owner. As he walked back he looked as normal as any mid 20's kid could look. Nikes, jeans, a t-shirt with a snowboard brand on it. "He's sending a flatbed," he said, closing the phone.

"Is he pissed?" I asked.

"Nah. He just wanted to know who was driving. I told him it was you," he answered laughing and sporting a prankish grin.

"Gosh, thanks," I said not knowing whether to believe him.

We leaned against the inert car.

"So, where were we?" he asked.

"The most fun you've had with a hack." He had been thinking this over when the Lamborghini's monstrous V12 engine decided it had had quite enough.

"That's hard to say because I try to make them all 'fun'. Even the state-sponsored stuff which can be creepy. But, from a pure amusement perspective, I'd have to say my first paid gig which came from an acquaintance of a professor at school. It wasn't hard because the target was fairly careless but the hunting, discovery and kill thrills were certainly there. I miss that rush. It was primal."

"Who was it for?" I asked

He looked over and laughed. "Really?"

I had to laugh too, but at myself for asking. "Ok, tell me what you can."

He thought a few moments then said, "I was hired by the CEO who was fairly certain somebody just below the C-suite was passing on the goods to a competitor in Europe."

"How did the CEO know?"

"The IT guys had discovered an unusually clever backdoor [a way into the servers that bypassed security] which they immediately patched. In retrospect they should have left it, and watched it, but by policy, they simply killed it. It was mentioned nominally later in a weekly memo to the corner offices."

"This was the heads up to the CEO?"

"Well, that's the thing. It was routine and he didn't give it much thought. Then the next week as he was walking down the hall to a conference room when he stopped into somebody's office to ask a question. Unfortunately, or fortunately, depending on your perspective, the guy was in the restroom. As the CEO waited he noticed the dude's notebook screen was displaying the TOR browser screen. The CEO had heard about TOR and had the presence of mind to check the browser's bookmarks for .onion sites and the only thing bookmarked was TOR mail." John paused a moment then asked, "You ever use the dark web?"

I nodded.

"Under what circumstances?" he asked.

"I've taken a couple assignments to locate and participate in hidden deep and dark web sites where pissed off employees were selling or swapping various forms of inside information."

"You ever use bitcoin?" John asked.

[Explanation: Bitcoin is a pseudo-anonymous digital currency often used to pay for goods and services on the deep web. If something is illegal to own, use your imagination here, you can probably buy it with bitcoin. Same with services. That said, plenty of legitimate companies are adopting it due to its natural security and low friction transfer properties.]

"I've been paid with them a couple times plus I ran an early mine. I've seen company secrets for sale priced in bitcoin. The dark web is a crazy place. It's the Wild West in there. Huge and spooky," I said.

"Exactly. So why would this guy be playing in there? Especially when he later insisted he simply stumbled across TOR.

I laughed. "Nobody simply 'stumbles' across TOR," I said. "Obviously he was up to something. The CEO probably made him right there with the BS."

"Well, at least there was now a possible explanation for some things a competitor had done," John said.

[Explanation: The TOR browser is used for anonymous web browsing and allows access to hidden parts of the web that most people don't even know exists called the "deep web". Used properly TOR provides near perfect anonymity while browsing by encrypting and bouncing your web page calls through servers all over the world. Along the same lines, TOR-based e-mail is almost impossible to trace back to its source if you stay in the TOR environment. Anti-regime political activists (e.g. Arab Spring) commonly use these tools as do criminals, disgruntled employees, etc.]

"Who owned the employee's computer?" I asked.

"The company."

"Why didn't they just take it and have a look? If it's clearly the company's property there is no realistic expectation of privacy."

"True but that would be too obvious. The CEO didn't want the guy to know he was being looked at until the right moment. That's when I came in because he couldn't task anyone in his company since it might get back to the well-liked guy and he would just try and destroy the evidence."

"So, what did you do?"

"I dropped some nice malware onto the computer and remotely had a look. The only thing suspicious was an encrypted volume that was hardly hidden and had an innocuous name. But you have to ask yourself, if the contents are innocuous why go to all the trouble to encrypt the file container? Why not just use a good password on the individual files. So I tried to brute force the container open but, of course, that's tough and can take a while. So with the client's permission I crashed the notebook hard enough so that after a couple days of trying to fix it himself the guy left it with the evening IT crew to fix, which they did. After they delivered it to the guy's office afterhours the CEO's trusted assistant picked it up and brought it into her office where I was waiting. And this is when it got seriously fun."

"How so?"

"Because it turned out this guy was a lot smarter than the CEO gave him credit for. When I took out the Vaio's battery there was a sticky note stuck to it. It said 'If found call such and such number'. Sure enough, with some jiggling of the spaces, that was the pass phrase that unlocked the file container. Initially I thought it was pretty lame...or really smart. I called the client and we reviewed the two files I found. Important design IP but not something you would protect beyond physical control of the notebook plus a decent password. But I had a hunch. I started looking everywhere for something else. I KNEW there had to be something else on the encrypted drive but I couldn't see it. It was driving me nuts."

"Maybe it was on a thumb drive someplace else. I've recovered locked USB drives and they can be a bitch and that's assuming you can even find them in the first place."

He smiled and pointed to me. "Close! What I figured he had done, or was done for him since it's tricky, was make the real files invisible. You know, make another container, a hidden one, within the one I had just busted open."

I nodded. "'Plausible deniability'. Nice!" I said, impressed.

"'Nice'? Are you kidding me? Back then I was a noob and thought it was freak'n awesome! Even if the guy was confronted by his boss all he had to do was give up the password to the in plain sight folder that everyone could see. Same thing in court under subpoena. You give up the passwords to files that are only 'just a little' embarrassing. It can be impossible to prove the real stuff even exists. It's just noise on the disk."

"What did you do to find the hidden volume? I thought that was impossible without the password?"

He laughed. "It pretty much is but I was on a roll and the guy was, in fact, an idiot. So on a hunch I did another brute force starting with the pass phrase he used to lock the first container. With the head start it was a trivial break and the files just suddenly appeared on the screen. I thought it was the coolest thing I had ever seen. I felt like a rock star. I learned later it was just his daughter's cell phone number. He just substituted it. Dumb. I was out of the place by 4AM. I had a great breakfast with the assistant. Best twelve hours of my life!"

I thought about this a moment then said, "Talk about being a noob. There were a hundred ways to do it better. He should have just put the stuff on an encrypted thumb drive and stashed the thing in his wife's lingerie draw. What was in the files?"

"Pretty much the company's DNA. He was the COO in perpetual waiting for the top spot. So he had everything and he was pissed."

"What happened to him?" I asked.

"After quietly signing a very long statement he was made available to other employers and, naturally, he went directly to work for the company he was piping the IP to."

I smiled. "Right. Let me guess who he REALLY works for."

John laughed, "Yep! You gotta love this valley. We've got more Bournes running around than Amazon!

I knew there was a lot more to the story but obviously it was a waste of time to ask. I leaned back against the car and looked up at the cerulean sky and the puffy clouds coming up from the coast. This had been fun.

A while later we headed down Woodside Road in the tow truck and had the driver drop us off at famous Buck's of Woodside for lunch.

Interesting day. *Perfect Day.*

WHAT YOU SHOULD BE DOING MINUTE TO MINUTE

Originally Published
Fall 2012

ASSIGNMENT: FT 500 COO candidate
LOCATION: Piazza San Marco, Venice, Italy
CLIENT: Global 500 company

We were sitting at a small round table on the side of the Piazza San Marco in Venice. The famous bell tower rose high above us. There were a lot of pigeons around. In a sudden, flapping flourish, several took off right over us.

The candidate, in his 50s, laughed as he ducked. We had been talking for about an hour. Time was running short and I was getting ready to turn off the small digital recorder on the table between us.

I turned back to the candidate. "Ok, one more question. This one is for my newsletter and if you don't mind we'll keep the recorder going. The rest of the interview I'll e-mail to the client from the airport before I leave tonight.

"Sure," he said holding up his espresso cup signaling the furtive waiter to bring another.

"Share with me your best tip. Something a true corporate warrior should know. Something that helped you get where you are, which is obviously a pretty good place despite your boss's scandal."

Before he could answer, a sharp comment in a language I didn't understand came from the next table. It was obviously cursing which has a nearly universal tone. The candidate and I both looked over. An elegant, well dressed blond woman was sitting alone, staring at a fresh white blotch on her navy blue jacket sleeve. A pigeon had made a deposit. I leaned over and placed my espresso spoon and carafe of water in front of her. "First the spoon and then all the water," I said smiling.

The candidate, with an understanding smile and enthusiasm that seemed to raise the day's fading light said, "And remember, it's good luck!"

Following the instructions she thanked us in what sounded Slavic, maybe Russian. But it didn't matter. Her eloquent smile said everything worth saying.

I turned back to the candidate. "So, your best tip for high-value managers. For true corporate warrior types."

"Ok," he said looking from the pretty woman back to me. "That's easy. You've come all this way to interview me because your client knows of me as someone who gets a lot done. People think it's a trick and it's not. It's a simple mindset. At any slack moment, I ask myself what is the most important thing I can be doing *right now*. Back when I started in Belgium my mentor taught me there is never enough time to do everything you have to do, but there is always enough time to do the most important thing."

"But how do you choose?" I asked as his espresso arrived.

"The easiest tells are things with long term consequences."

As he finished the espresso we both looked at our watches. "We good?" he asked.

I nodded, put a colorful Euro note down and picked up the recorder as we both stood up, returning the warm smile from the woman at the next table. "We're good," I said shaking his hand.

With that he strolled off towards his wife and daughter waiting at nearby Harry's Bar. As I watched him I asked myself what was the most important thing I should be doing right then. The answer was pretty simple: I picked up my light carry-on and headed toward the Grand Canal and the ferry ride to Marco Polo Airport for the evening flight to Istanbul and the next candidate.

More later…

WHAT'S YOUR STIRRUP?

Originally Published
Fall 2012

ASSIGNMENT: FT 500 COO candidate (succession planning)
LOCATION: Istanbul, Turkey
CLIENT: Global 500 company

After the walk down from the hotel in Istanbul the candidate and I took a seat on a bench overlooking the river-like Bosporus. Although we were sitting in Europe, we could see Asia not even two miles across the water. Ferryboats and other boat traffic were busily moving back and forth in front of us. To the right was the Sea of Marmara leading to the Aegean and up the Bosporus to the left was the Black Sea less than 20 miles away. Across the water from us, I could see tall minarets of mosques glowing in the fading orange light. The air was warm and moist. Another early evening in a beguiling place proving, once again, serious recruiting can still be enjoyable.

The secret interview up at the Ritz Carlton had gone well and turned into a long, multi-stop lunch as the candidate and I wandered through town to the water talking as we went. Editing down the recorded sections of the conversation for the client was going to be a complex chore back at the hotel, when my head cleared. And it definitely had clearing to do thanks to some very strange raki and ouzo based concoctions we had consumed as we wandered around while I got to know him.

"That's my ride," the candidate said pointing from the shore to a white speck racing across the straits directly toward us.

"So, what's your secret?" I asked watching the approaching, cigarette-style boat. It was hard to judge its speed but I figured we had about two minutes. I could already hear its big, meaty engines.

The candidate turned on the bench to face me. "Secrets?" he said laughing. "I have no secrets. What makes you think I have secrets?"

"Your effectiveness," I said simply. "What makes you so effective?"

He thought about it a moment. I noticed this habit earlier. He didn't just flip out an answer like most candidates hoping to impress. When I tossed a question mark at him it was as if he would catch it and examine it carefully for a moment before answering. It was refreshing to watch.

He finally said, "I guess it would be my ability to recognize how well a person uses his or her stirrup."

Now it was my turn to pause, trying to figure it out. "You mean as in a, horse?" I asked, baffled.

"Right. Every successful manager has a stirrup. The question is what is it, and how well do they use it."

"I'm still not following you."

"It's simple. A big reason Genghis Kahn conquered so much of the world was because of his expert use of horses. The horses were, in effect, the terror weapon of their day. Even better than the earlier chariot which was expensive to build. But until the invention of the stirrup, the horse as a weapons platform had a serious flaw. The rider was so busy hanging on for dear life he couldn't accurately aim his distance weapons which were heavy crossbow arrows. The stirrup changed that. Now the warrior could not only move fast but could accurately aim his weapon at the same time. Combined with Kahn's tactics it was a key advantage and a game changer."

We both looked over at the approaching speedboat, which now appeared to glow red in the setting sunlight.

I looked back at the candidate. "You're describing concentration of force and that's a great thing if you know where to focus it."

"And a good manager does," he said as we stood up. "That's part of their job."

"Of course," I said as we walked toward a stubby little pier where the launch had pulled up. "But I'm still waiting for you to relate your success to stirrups."

He laughed as he took a long, steady step down into the rocking boat. "Very simple. As we discussed at lunch, in business it's hard to do something truly meaningful entirely alone. You need a great team. So when I'm thinking about hiring somebody I look to see if they have a stirrup. And if so, can I use it to help change the game to the sustainable benefit of the ownership. Keep me posted," he said looking up and waving goodbye. With that, he leaned into the powerful boat's acceleration as it roared off to his shoreside home across the straits.

I watched as the boat got smaller, then could hear the engines change note as it started a wide sweeping turn to the left and head back towards me. My phone buzzed signaling a text message.

"We're coming back to pick you up. I'm having dinner with somebody you should meet."

This will be interesting, I thought to myself waiting for the approaching boat.

ADVICE FROM A MYSTERIOUS RUSSIAN

Originally Published
Fall 2012

ASSIGNMENT: FT 500 COO candidate (succession planning), Part 2
LOCATION: Istanbul, Turkey
CLIENT: Global 500 company

While waiting on the dock here in Istanbul something weird is in the air.

As an executive recruiter that has never said no to a tough, unlikely assignment I've found myself in many a strange situation. Done right, proper recruiting is an intoxicating blend of hunting and sales. Find The Best and sell them on your client. Fill the empty seat. The quant dogs of BCG can take their number rush; I'll take a tough search assignment any day. At least that's what I was reminding myself of…

With evening quickly fading to night I jumped down into the big speedboat. No sooner had I grabbed onto one of the high seats than the driver cracked open the throttles and the hellacious engines roared up to full voice and we took off up the Bosporus. The 50's candidate I interviewed throughout the afternoon looked over at me and smiled. I didn't know who we were going to meet. It was spur of the moment. I have the generally useful trait of being up for almost anything.

I had arrived late last night into Istanbul and this afternoon met up with the COO succession candidate for a lunch that turned into a pleasant multi-stop food ramble through town. It was going well. He understood my client's challenges and shared his own thinking about them. He was on board, very sharp, and connected. He was happy to let me record most of the conversation and the audio quality was good. I was looking forward to getting back to the hotel to edit it down and transmit it to the client.

Well, that was the plan anyway. But now we were slowing up to a dock by the candidate's waterside villa. We tied up next to an old fishing boat that looked out of place against the beautiful houses overlooking the water. There was something odd about the wooden boat but I couldn't put my finger on it. It seemed very clean for a fishing trawler.

I climbed up onto the dock and looked over my shoulder across the strait to downtown Istanbul. I could see the colorful safety of my tall hotel. That was Europe. Although still in Istanbul, we were now walking in Asia. It felt darker, and it wasn't just the fading orange light.

As we approached the sliding glass doors behind a beautiful, faintly modern house, the candidate turned around and said, "I've told my friend you're the guy whose newsletter I occasionally forward. You're both in the people business. He's semi-retired. Don't ask him a lot of questions."

This didn't help my comfort level. I ask questions for a living.

As we walked into a formal, dark wood paneled room a short, heavyset man in an old fisherman sweater got up and shook the candidate's hand, then mine. His hand was massive and could have easily crumbled mine like a graham cracker. He was introduced simply as Yuri by the candidate. I was introduced with both my first and last name. The man smiled and nodded, somehow knowingly. It was obviously his boat out back. They smelled the same.

"The ladies are upstairs in the kitchen with the fish I brought," Yuri said in a gravelly voice that sounded like Henry Kissinger but with the stretched out syllables of Russian.

"Great. You two have a seat," the candidate said as he disappeared around a corner.

Yuri and I sat down. On the table between us was a chilled screw cap bottle without the cap, three stubby wine glasses and a bowl of pickles. I could smell vodka. I knew what was coming. My head hurt already from the afternoon. We made small talk about fishing, subtly testing each other's answer depth. Despite the sweater the place smelled great. Somebody knows how to cook fish, I thought to myself.

When the candidate came down we all sipped, then tossed back the chilled vodka. It was strangely smooth. There was no burn at all. Nice.

Yuri reached across to get the bottle. As he did the left sleeve of the worn sweater slid up. In the overhead light I caught a glimpse of the distinctive octagonal face of a massively expensive gold Audemars Piguet Royal Oak watch. His business, whatever it really is, must be good.

Another round went down. Number two. It was hitting me.

There was a strange dynamic in the room. The three of us formed an equal sided triangle, with the host at the end of the table, but clearly I was on the outside. I wanted to somehow take back some control but I knew it simply wasn't possible—I never had any to give up. The Russian controlled the room. It was like he controlled the gravity holding us all to the floor. He was like Jack Welch in his prime at GE. The Russian's human capital was immense. You could feel it. People around him became his property, willing or not.

Yuri looked from me to the host and asked. "You told him about finding someone's stirrup??"

"He did," I said answering the question for him.

"I've read some of your rules. Some are useful," the fisherman said to me.

"And which ones have you found 'useful'?" I asked breaking the host's no questions rule.

The Russian thought a moment, looking down at his vodka glass then back over to me. "The ones about controlling the movements of your enemy or competition. Mostly good stuff." He paused, then repeated, smiling, "Mostly." He reached down and picked one of the pickles out of the bowl and bit it in half. It crunched.

"What would you add?" I asked. "What's a management rule that's worked for you?" I glanced over to our host who seemed OK with the question. I realized it was the identity of the Russian I wasn't supposed to poke around. That was OK with me. Eventually I would find out. I always do.

While Yuri was thinking the host reached over and refilled the glasses. The three of us tossed them back. That was it for me. I had to work later on the day's recordings. Tough to do when a room won't stay still around you.

The Russian spoke. "Well, you should certainly never let anyone know the reality of how hard you are working on something. It just needs to get done."

"And why is that?" I asked.

"The moment somebody knows how hard you are working they can measure more precisely what you are capable of. That is not good. They know your limits and can predict your behavior. In my experience, it is better to make everything look effortless, even if you are withering, and then choose more wisely, later, if you misjudged."

I said, "That's the old corporate warfare rule of controlling your competition by controlling what they think they know about you. War and business, it's largely the same."

"Exactly," the fisherman said. "My first mentor taught me how to move arrogant or unskilled enemies around like chess pieces by making them think something I was doing was either very tough, or very easy, or something in-between. It's gratifying to watch your enemy do exactly what you intend them to do. Disinformation is a cheap yet very powerful weapon."

"When weak, appear strong. When strong, appear weak," I said.

Watching me closely he finished my thought saying, "When close, appear far. When far, appear close." Still watching me he paused then added slowly, "Scientia est potentia."

"'Knowledge is power'," I answered nodding and smiling inside, translating the Latin.

A few seconds of silence followed as we watched each other, then a woman's voice came from upstairs. The host made a gesture with his hand and a moment later the glass door behind me slid open. The boat driver stood outside waiting, obviously for me. Whatever this was, it was over. Our host stood up, with Yuri and me following.

The fisherman reached out to shake my hand. "Tell me Mr. Newhart," he said shaking it. "Why is it a bad idea to be just as good as your competition?"

At last, new fruit to pluck. "Because, Yuri, 'as good' means average," I said. "There's nothing compelling about average; it's just another word for mediocre. Nobody changes for mediocre. They change for better. That's why I came all this way to talk to him," I said nodding toward the candidate who was a great example of better.

I thanked our host and stepped halfway out the door but stopped when the fisherman spoke. "It was nice finally meeting you. Our paths will cross again."

"I know," I said before turning out the door into the moist night air. That's when I realized I was being interviewed for something.

The next day I flew home to Chicago. It had been an interesting few days.

Think about it...

ENSURING CORPORATE VICTORY BY USING OODA LOOPS

Originally Published
June 2014

SUBJECT: Better decision making with OODA loops. Bitcoin adventures.
ASSIGNMENT: Find a knowledgeable (and trustworthy) cryptocurrency consultant
CLIENT: A large venture capital firm

I'm sitting on a bench by Claw Fountain in White Plaza at Stanford University and entering this directly into a tablet while it's fresh in my mind since I was asked to not record the interview. It's the final interview for a cryptocurrency consultant position, focusing on Bitcoin. (This is the third cryptocurrency interviewing or recruiting assignment in the last 4 months alone.) It was an interesting discussion as we did the fountain walk and not just because it involved bitcoin. I've been involved with cryptocurrency for a few years now and, in fact, funded a small 'mining' operation for bitcoins back when simple graphics cards could economically solve the complex equations required to create the currency and run the underlying bitcoin ecosystem. In addition, I've been paid in bitcoin for services (an interesting story in itself…). There's no longer any question about it, peer-to-peer cryptocurrencies like bitcoin have some very interesting, and useful, properties in today's overstressed global economy, not to mention the banking world.

However, as interesting as largely unregulable cryptocurrencies are in an age of aggressive global quantitative easing by the central banks (unnerving), there was an aspect of our conversations that I found even more engaging. The candidate had been a fighter pilot and he used those skills as a basis for his decision-making skills which are remarkable in their speed and accuracy across all subjects and tasks. I asked him to reduce it to some usable details that I said I would share with my Corpwar readers, of which he has been a member for over 10 years.

He explained that in the Korean conflict the US flew the F-86 Sabre jet against the MiG-15. The MiG-15 was clearly a superior aircraft on paper (more thrust, speed, etc.). Yet the Americans had air superiority with a ~10:1 kill ratio over the MiG, meaning we shot down 10 of them for each one of ours shot down. Training played a role in this but it could not, alone, explain the extreme ratio. So, what was going on and how does this apply to conducting modern business?

It took a fighter pilot and mathematician to figure it out. It largely came down to basic aircraft canopy design. The Sabre jet had a bubble canopy providing the pilot a better view of the airspace environment. The MiG's canopy was much more enclosed, limiting the pilot's peripheral view of the surrounding environment (note: this was largely before electronic threat detection but the principle is the same—today's electronics extend the pilot's 'view' of threats, expanding his or her ability to observe). There was another advantage in that the Sabre jet's hydraulics responded very slightly quicker to the pilot's control inputs than the MiG's. So while the Sabre couldn't turn as tight a radius, it could get *into* the turn quicker.

The two advantages were lethal to the enemy, or, relative to my readers, your corporate competition. In very broad strokes, here is the resulting rule and what it's called: The party that can **OBSERVE** the situation, **ORIENT** to it, **DECIDE** what to do about it, and take appropriate **ACTION** will typically win. This is the basis of the 'OODA loop' or OODA cycle and it had a tremendous impact on military thinking.

It all gets down to speed. You need to get 'inside' a competitor's decision cycle. The Sabre's bubble canopy allowed the pilots to see, or observe, MiGs sooner and the American jet's faster responding hydraulics allowed the pilot to implement Action quicker. Orienting and Deciding come with training and experience but you must see what's going on and be able to implement your reaction. Thus, the Sabre's 10:1 advantage in the skies over Korea.

There's much more to it than that, such as changing the environment quicker than your competition can react, or even comprehend, then promptly exploiting his confused and hasty decisions, but this outline is the usable, leverageable gist for the action oriented corporate warrior.

So, speed through the OODA loop. Think about it. We all use OODA loops whether we know it or not. The trick is to do it quicker than your competition.

If you get your team thinking formally in these terms (Observing, Orienting, Deciding and Acting), allowing them to get inside your competition's corresponding OODA cycle, you will hammer them almost every time, especially if they have a cumbersome, meeting-heavy corporate culture.

Always be thinking: How can I get INSIDE my competition's turning circle? This will confuse him since he is responding to old information; the way things *were*, not the way they *are*. During this phase you own them.

That's how you win for your equity holders; that's how you win for yourself.

Think about it…

ABOUT TAL NEWHART &
THE ART OF CORPORATE WARFARE

Tal Newhart is a successful senior executive recruiter, interviewer and special projects advisor. This book is a collection of newsletters and blog posts he sent to his clients, candidates and friends over the span of 13 years starting in 2002 in the wake of Enron and WorldCom. Although occasionally controversial, the newsletters were often forwarded by business leaders to their internal contact lists to help their managers compete more effectively in an increasingly competitive and recession plagued marketplace.

Created as an informal tool to help his clients and fellow entrepreneurs throw curveballs at their competition, The Art of Corporate Warfare adapts the ground tactics of famous battles to win battles in the modern marketplace. Also included are useful conversations, interviews and experiences that helped Newhart form the ethos of the modern 'corporate warrior,' a useful topic on which he is a decidedly pointed corporate speaker.

What is a 'corporate warrior'? As Newhart puts it, "Simple. An employee whose only goal is to lawfully, and sustainably, increase the value of the company that is paying them."

This collection supplies techniques and philosophies to help readers achieve that goal.

Thanks for reading my book. I've given you a lot to think about. Now go kick some ass every single day!

www.ingramcontent.com/pod-product-compliance
Lightning Source LLC
Chambersburg PA
CBHW030939180526
45163CB00002B/631